m L

JAN - - 2014

The FDA & Psychiatric Drugs: How a Drug Is Approved

THE STATE OF
MENTAL ILLNESS
AND ITS THERAPY

THE STATE OF MENTAL ILLNESS AND ITS THERAPY

The FDA & Psychiatric Drugs:
How a Drug Is Approved

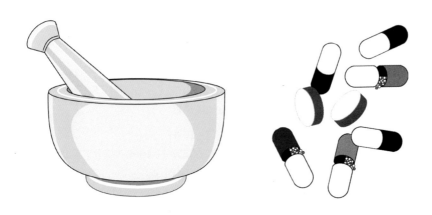

Joan Esherick

Mason Crest

Mason Crest
450 Parkway Drive, Suite D
Broomall, PA 19008
www.masoncrest.com

Printed in the Hashemite Kingdom of Jordan.

First printing
9 8 7 6 5 4 3 2 1

Series ISBN: 978-1-4222-2819-7
ISBN: 978-1-4222-2826-5
ebook ISBN: 978-1-4222-8987-7

The Library of Congress has cataloged the
hardcopy format(s) as follows:

Library of Congress Cataloging-in-Publication Data

Esherick, Joan.
  [FDA and psychiatric drugs]
  The FDA & psychiatric drugs : how a drug is approved / Joan Esherick.
     pages cm. – (The state of mental illness and its therapy)
  Revision of: The FDA and psychiatric drugs, 2004.
  Audience: 12.
  Audience: Grade 7 to 8.
  Includes index.
  ISBN 978-1-4222-2826-5 (hardcover) – ISBN 978-1-4222-2819-7 (series) – ISBN 978-1-4222-8987-7 (ebook)
  1. Psychotropic drugs–Testing–Law and legislation–United States–Juvenile literature. 2. Drug approval–United States–Juvenile literature. 3. Mental illness–Chemotherapy–Juvenile literature. 4. United States. Food and Drug Administration–Juvenile literature. I. Title. II. Title: FDA and psychiatric drugs. III. Title: Food and Drug Administration & psychiatric drugs.
  RM315.E74 2014
  615.7'88–dc23
                          2013008197

Produced by Vestal Creative Services.
www.vestalcreative.com

This book is meant to educate and should not be used as an alternative to appropriate medical care. Its creators have made every effort to ensure that the information presented is accurate—but it is not intended to substitute for the help and services of trained professionals.

Picture Credits:
Artville: pp. 15, 82, 102, 103, 104. Autumn Libal: p. 110. Benjamin Stewart: pp. 23, 25, 26. 63. Choosemyplate.gov: p. 98. Comstock: pp. 44, 47, 49, 50, 54, 59, 60, 64, 66, 73, 75, 77, 84, 91, 122. Corbis: pp. 86, 89, 108. Edyta Pawlowska | Dreamstime.com: p. 95. Kansas State Historical Society: p. 34. National Library of Medicine: pp. 17, 18, 20, 30, 36, 42, 115, 117, 118, 119, 120. Photo Alto: pp. 10, 12, 68. Photo Disc: pp. 94, 96, 101, 123. Stockbyte: p. 112. The individuals in these images are models, and the images are for illustrative purposes only. The individuals in these images are models, and the images are for illustrative purposes only. To the best knowledge of the publisher, all other images are in the public domain. If any image has been inadvertently uncredited or miscredited, please notify Vestal Creative Services, Vestal, New York 13850, so that rectification can be made for future printings.

CONTENTS

Introduction
by Mary Ann McDonnell

Teenagers have reason to be interested in psychiatric disorders and their treatment. Friends, family members, and even teens themselves may experience one of these disorders. Using scenarios adolescents will understand, this series explains various psychiatric disorders and the drugs that treat them.

Diagnosis and treatment of psychiatric disorders in children between six and eighteen years old are well studied and documented in the scientific journals. A paper appearing in the *Journal of the American Academy of Child and Adolescent Psychiatry* in 2010 estimated that 49.5 percent of all adolescents aged 13 to 18 were affected by at least one psychiatric disorder. Various other studies have reported similar findings. Needless to say, many children and adolescents are suffering from psychiatric disorders and are in need of treatment.

Many children have more than one psychiatric disorder, which complicates their diagnoses and treatment plans. Psychiatric disorders often occur together. For instance, a person with a sleep disorder may also be depressed; a teenager with attention-deficit/hyperactivity disorder (ADHD) may also have a substance-use disorder. In psychiatry, we call this comorbidity. Much research addressing this issue has led to improved diagnosis and treatment.

The most common child and adolescent psychiatric disorders are anxiety disorders, depressive disorders, and ADHD. Sleep disorders, sexual disorders, eating disorders, substance-abuse disorders, and psychotic disorders are also quite common. This series has volumes that address each of these disorders.

Major depressive disorders have been the most commonly diagnosed mood disorders for children and adolescents. Researchers don't agree as to how common mania and bipolar disorder are in children. Some experts believe that manic episodes in children and adolescents are underdiagnosed. Many times, a mood disturbance may occur with another psychiatric disorder. For instance, children with ADHD may also be depressed. ADHD is just one psychiatric disorder that is a major health concern for children, adolescents, and adults. Studies of ADHD have reported prevalence rates among children that range from two to 12 percent.

Failure to understand or seek treatment for psychiatric disorders puts children and young adults at risk of developing substance-use disorders. For example, recent research indicates that those with ADHD who were treated with medication were 85 percent less likely to develop a substance-use disorder. Results like these emphasize the importance of timely diagnosis and treatment.

Early diagnosis and treatment may prevent these children from developing further psychological problems. Books like those in this series provide important information, a vital first step toward increased awareness of psychological disorders; knowledge and understanding can shed light on even the most difficult subject. These books should never, however, be viewed as a substitute for professional consultation. Psychiatric testing and an evaluation by a licensed professional is recommended to determine the needs of the child or adolescent and to establish an appropriate treatment plan.

Foreword
by Donald Esherick

We live in a society filled with technology—from computers surfing the Internet to automobiles operating on gas and batteries. In the midst of this advanced society, diseases, illnesses, and medical conditions are treated and often cured with the administration of drugs, many of which were unknown thirty years ago. In the United States, we are fortunate to have an agency, the Food and Drug Administration (FDA), which monitors the development of new drugs and then determines whether the new drugs are safe and effective for use in human beings.

When a new drug is developed, a pharmaceutical company usually intends that drug to treat a single disease or family of diseases. The FDA reviews the company's research to determine if the drug is safe for use in the population at large and if it effectively treats the targeted illnesses. When the FDA finds that the drug is safe and effective, it approves the drug for treating that specific disease or condition. This is called the labeled indication.

During the routine use of the drug, the pharmaceutical company and physicians often observe that a drug treats other medical conditions besides what is indicated in the labeling. While the labeling will not include the treatment of the particular condition, a physician can still prescribe the drug to a patient with this disease. This is known as an unlabeled or off-label indication. This series contains information about both the labeled and off-label indications of psychiatric drugs.

I have reviewed the books in this series from the perspective of the pharmaceutical industry and the FDA, specifically focusing on the labeled indications, uses, and known side effects of these drugs. Further information can be found on the FDA's website (www.FDA.gov).

A person with one kind of psychiatric disorder may be obsessed with the feeling that her hands are dirty. Psychiatric drugs can alleviate these feelings.

Chapter One

Psychiatric Drugs: What Are They and How Do They Work?

Thirteen-year-old Sarah's morning was anything but ordinary. The minute she awoke, she shot out of bed and rushed to the shower to rid herself of the awful germs she feared had contaminated her while she slept.

"Lather, scrub, rinse, *one*. Lather, scrub, rinse, *two*. Lather, scrub rinse, *three*," she chanted as she washed. Sarah shampooed and rinsed twenty-one times. She washed her face twenty-one times. She scrubbed each arm, leg, and foot twenty-one times.

The ritual repeated itself when Sarah brushed her teeth, and yet again when she combed her hair. Twenty-one strokes: no more, no less.

ritual: An act or series of acts that is repeated formally and customarily.

With teeth gleaming and hair brushed, Sarah continued her "twenty-ones" by shaking the germs from her clothes: twenty-one shakes each for her underwear, sweater, jeans, socks, and shoes. If she forgot to count or was interrupted, she started all over again. It had to be twenty-one. It always had to be twenty-one.

Sarah was convinced that twenty-one was her magic number; doing routine things twenty-one times would keep her safe from harm. But Sarah's "twenty-ones" (up from the "threes" she had used earlier in her life) demanded more and more time from her each day. The lengthening ritual interfered with everyday life, but Sarah just couldn't stop. Her morning routine, once only a few minutes, had grown to nearly three hours.

Someone like Jeremy may be unable to focus on life.

Fifteen-year-old Jeremy's day began very differently. Instead of shooting out of bed as Sarah did, Jeremy lingered. His mom prodded him to get up, waking him over and over again. She constantly nagged him about showering and wearing clean clothes, but he didn't care. He wasn't concerned about his looks, or about what other people thought. He was convinced that most people didn't really care about him, and most of the time he was either angry, irritable, or wanted to cry.

When Jeremy finally did get up, his brain seemed shrouded with fog, like he was lost in a haze. He found it difficult to think or focus on any one thing. *Why go to school if I can't concentrate?* Jeremy often thought. *I can't seem to do anything right anymore. Everybody hates me anyway.* Jeremy craved sleep and had little energy, even for things he used to enjoy. He just wanted the world, and everyone in it, to leave him alone.

Perhaps you've known someone like Sarah or Jeremy. Perhaps you see something of yourself in their stories. Though their experiences seem very different, Jeremy and Sarah share two things in common: they both suffer from a psychological disorder and they are not alone.

Psychological Disorders: What Are They?

You've heard it before: "She's nuts." "He's got to be crazy." "What's wrong with that kid, anyway?" "He's psycho!" We throw those terms around carelessly, but psychological disorders are much more common than we think. The National Institute of Mental Health (NIMH) suggests that one in four Americans suffers from a diagnosable psychological disorder in any given year.

mental illness: General term used to describe psychological conditions that affect a person's ability to think, feel, or act appropriately.

schizophrenia: A psychological disorder that causes a person to confuse what is real with what is imaginary. Hallucinations and delusions are common symptoms of schizophrenia.

Look around you. Think of four friends or four other people you know. In all probability, one will end up with a psychological disorder. It could be you. Do you take classes with thirty other students? Seven are likely candidates for mental illness. According to the World Health Organization, of the top ten causes of disability worldwide, four are psychological disorders. In developed countries, they are the leading cause.

What are psychological disorders? Psychological disorders (also called mental disorders) are a type of mental illness, which affects a person's ability to think, feel, or behave appropriately. When a person doesn't function normally, when he can't communicate or interact with people appropriately, when she doesn't take care of herself or her personal hygiene, when he can't perform his job, complete his school work, or just isn't himself anymore—he or she may be suffering from a psychological disorder. These disorders can affect anyone regardless of age, gender, race, nationality, or social status. Adults can have psychological disorders; children and teens can have them, too.

Many psychological disorders have been depicted in the movies or on TV. The 1975 award-winning classic *One Flew Over the Cuckoo's Nest*, starring Jack Nicholson, portrayed a variety of disorders as it examined life in a psychiatric hospital. *Blue Sky*, the 1994 release for which actress Jessica Lange won an Academy Award, examined the life of a woman with bipolar disorder. The 2001 release, *A Beautiful Mind*, is based on the true story of Nobel Prize–winning mathematician, John Forbes Nash Jr. (played by Russell Crowe), who struggled to overcome schizophrenia, another well-

Psychiatrists work to understand what goes on within the human brain.

known mental disorder. And the television series *Monk* portrays a detective with obsessive-compulsive disorder (OCD)—the same disorder that drove Sarah's twenty-one routine.

If you haven't seen them in the movies or on TV, you've probably heard of these common psychological disorders: mood disorders (depression or bipolar disorder), panic attacks, attention-deficit/hyperactivity disorder (ADHD), post-traumatic stress disorder (PTSD), or autism (a type of pervasive developmental disorder).

Psychological disorders come in many shapes and sizes and can affect

depression: A mental illness characterized by long-term sadness.

bipolar disorder: A mental illness characterized by periods of extreme "highs" and extreme "lows."

panic attacks: Sudden feelings of extreme fear, often immobilizing.

psychiatrists: Medical doctors (MDs) who specialize in diagnosing, treating, and preventing mental illnesses and substance use disorders. A psychiatrist can write prescriptions for medicines.

diagnosis: The medical opinion reached after identifying the nature and cause of a patient's disease or injury. A diagnosis is reached by examining the patient, the patient's history, and the patient's medical test results.

tic disorder: Involuntary movements or speech.

people very differently. To identify and classify these disabilities, psychiatrists rely on the *Diagnostic and Statistical Manual of Mental Disorders*, fourth edition, text revision (DSM-IV-TR), which is a book put out by the American Psychiatric Association that lists all known psychological disorders, their symptoms, and methods of treatment. This reference manual also lists criteria for the doctor to make a diagnosis. The criteria are lists of symptoms doctors can use as checklists; if a patient's symptoms match a checklist, the doctor knows which psychological disorder the patient has and how to treat him.

Symptoms of psychological disorders range from mild to debilitating and can be most unsettling to experience or see. Imagine if the person sitting next to you right now began to sniff and clear her throat over and over again. What if she began to make strange sounds or utter unintelligible words? What if she couldn't help herself no matter how much you asked her to stop or how hard she tried? Would you feel uncomfortable, nervous, or afraid? Maybe you'd laugh.

But what if it were you? What if you suddenly felt your face twitching, or your shoulders shrugging, and you couldn't control your movements? What if you heard sounds coming out of your mouth you couldn't believe were coming from you? What if you just couldn't stop? Would you laugh then or would it frighten you?

Both scenarios describe symptoms of a tic disorder, a lesser-

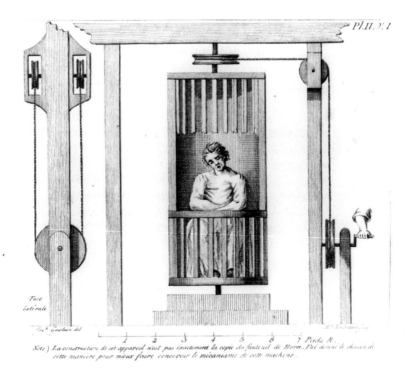

Long-ago treatments for psychological disorders were sometimes bizarre, as was this contraption designed to cure insanity.

known type of psychological disorder. In both cases you may have felt frightened or confused. That kind of reaction is normal for someone who has a psychological disorder and for those who know or love someone who struggles with one. But those feelings shouldn't prevent you from seeking help. Why? As Dr. Steven Hyman, a former director of the National Institute of Mental Health, once noted, "Mental illnesses are brain diseases . . . just as a stroke or a tumor is a brain disease." Because psychiatric disorders are diseases, many of today's drugs and therapies can safely and effectively treat even the most extreme forms.

The severest forms of mental illness cause people to do and say bizarre things because these people often confuse what is real with what is imaginary. Persons with more challenging disorders can hear imaginary voices, see imaginary people, or believe they are someone they are not. Doctors describe these patients as psychotic or as suffering from psychosis. But psychosis is part of only some mental illnesses. Most psychological disorders do not include psychosis, although this is what you often see portrayed in the movies. Many men, women, boys, and girls with diagnosable mental illnesses lead productive, happy lives without experiencing psychotic episodes.

The National Alliance for the Mentally Ill recognizes several famous people, both historical and contemporary, who lived (or are living) productive lives but wrestled with mental illness: Isaac Newton (physicist), Abraham Lincoln (U.S. president), Ludwig van Beethoven (classical composer), Vincent Van Gogh (Impressionist artist), Ernest Hemingway (novelist), Lionel Aldridge (football player for the Green Bay Packers), Jimmy Piersall (baseball player for the Boston Red Sox), and Patty Duke (Academy Award–winning actress), among others. Each suffered from a mental illness, though most knew little about its cause or cure.

We know more today. Much of what we know about psychological disorders was discovered in the last 150 years, but mental illnesses have been documented for centuries.

Psychological Disorders in History

Archaeologists have discovered evidences of mental illness as early as 10,000 BCE. Skulls unearthed at archaeological sites from that time indicate that early surgeries were performed on people with mental illness. (And yes, many even survived the procedure, only to have the surgery repeated again and again.) Ancient documents from the middle of the first century (36–68 CE) recount the bizarre, unpredictable behavior of Nero, the Roman Emperor who is best known for supposedly fiddling while Rome burned. Historians describe Nero as psychologically unstable, and he eventually committed suicide.

During the Middle Ages, the mentally ill were subjected to several strange practices thought to help them: bleeding, purging, flogging, and starvation (to starve out the evil spirits). Some died.

Not all historical references to the mentally ill describe such cruelty. A sixteenth-century German physician, Johannes Weyer, known for his kind treatment of those with psychological disorders, believed that his patients were not witches or possessed by the devil. He believed they were sick. In eighteenth-century France, Dr. Phillipe Pinel allowed the mentally ill to be freed from chains and other restraints and encouraged them to get fresh air and exercise. In the mid-1800s, a Massachusetts schoolteacher, Dorothea Dix, became a great force for reform of the treatment of the mentally ill when she alerted the state legislature to the horrific conditions under which the mentally ill lived. Dix worked for forty years to improve conditions and treatment of those with mental disorders. Unfortunately, these people were rare voices of sympathy for those who were outcast, chained, or abandoned by society. Theirs were also the voices of progress. We know today that most psychological disorders are a type of sickness, most commonly a sickness of the brain.

bleeding: The practice of treating the mentally ill by placing leeches on the patient's skin and allowing them to suck blood from the patient.

purging: A treatment method of the Middle Ages in which the patient was made to vomit or was given laxatives to rid him of evil spirits.

flogging: Whipping the patient to drive out the demons believed to cause mental illness.

In past centuries, people with psychological disorders were often kept bound.

What Causes Psychological Disorders?

Experts believe that mental disorders stem from problems in the brain's structure or chemistry. For example, the brain's chemical makeup can cause psychological disorders when it produces too much or too little of the chemicals it needs to function normally. This imbalance of brain chemicals is called a biochemical cause of mental illness. But biochemical causes aren't the only reasons for psychological disorders.

The brain may possess the right mix of chemicals, but be injured in other ways: in a bicycle or auto accident, by a stroke or birth defect, or from drug abuse or overdose.

biochemical: A cause of psychological disorders that has to do with brain chemistry.

Consider the case of railway foreman Phineas Gage. In 1848, Gage and his crew were preparing to lay railroad tracks for the new train that would run near Cavendish, Vermont. Using explosives to clear the land, Gage accidentally set off a charge too soon. The resulting explosion blew a tamping iron (an iron rod, three and a half feet long and an inch in diameter) through his head. The rod entered Gage's face near his left cheekbone, traveled through his brain and skull, and exited through the top of his head.

Amazingly, although most of the left half of his brain was destroyed, Phineas Gage survived. After months of medical care, he eventually returned to work for the railroads. But he was not the same man. Once friendly and easygoing, Phineas Gage had become agitated and foulmouthed. His brain injury resulted in a complete change of personality.

Gage's accident and resulting personality change helped scientists and doctors understand that brain injury can affect our emotions, behaviors, and personalities. His experience provided living proof of the link between physical injury and a psychological change. But there are other causes.

Acute sickness or chronic disease, like Alzheimer's or Parkinson's, can damage the brain and result in psychological disorders. Extreme stress, the loss of a loved one, a traumatic event, or other environmental factors can also trigger mental illness. Some psychological disorders come from something else entirely; they may pass from parent to child, from generation to generation. They may be genetic.

genetic: Being passed down from generation to generation through a family's genes.

Scientists and researchers have identified connections between all of these causes (biochemistry, brain injury, environmental factors, and genetics) and the resulting psychological disorders, but much is still unknown about the brain and how it functions. The brain has been called today's "last great frontier" because so much of the brain and how it works remains a mystery. Yet, what scientists do know, what they have discovered over the last century, can help us better understand psychological disorders, their causes, and how psychiatric drug treatments work.

The Brain and Psychological Disorders

Today we know that the brain is the body's control center, much like a hard drive is for a computer. Unlike most personal computers, however, the brain operates twenty-four hours a day. It controls everything we do: it sends messages to our lungs to tell them to expand for the next breath; it signals our hands when something is too hot or too cold; it triggers our emotional responses (prompts us to feel sad, angry, happy, or afraid) and it makes it possible for us to think. We can solve problems, imagine the future, make decisions,

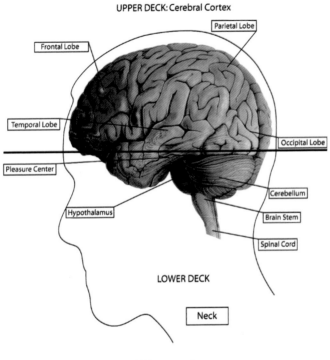

UPPER DECK: Cerebral Cortex

Parietal Lobe

Frontal Lobe

Temporal Lobe

Occipital Lobe

Pleasure Center

Cerebellum

Hypothalamus

Brain Stem

Spinal Cord

LOWER DECK

Neck

Figure 1

and choose certain actions—all because of our brains.

You could say that the brain is structured like a double-decker bus you might see in London, England. It has two main decks: the upper deck and lower deck. Just as the lower deck of a double-decker bus drives the vehicle, the brain's lower deck "drives" us to survive. This lower deck controls our basic needs and desires for things like food, reproduction, and rest. It is made up of three parts (see Figure 1): the brain stem, the pleasure center, and the hypothalamus. The brain stem and hypothalamus fuel our desire to satisfy basic survival needs. They drive us to eat, sleep, and procreate. When we get what we need, the pleasure center responds by making us feel satisfied.

> procreate: To reproduce; to create offspring.

Our double-decker brains also have an upper deck called the cerebral cortex. Just as a bus's upper deck is higher than its lower deck, the cerebral cortex is responsible for our "higher" thinking and motor skills: learning and remembering, obtaining and evaluating information, imagining and decision making, walking and talking.

The cerebral cortex consists of four main lobes, each having its own function. The frontal lobe, in the front half of the cerebral cortex, is responsible for our ability to move, think, pay attention, understand, and have social restraint (inhibitions). The parietal lobe, located behind the frontal lobe, processes our sense of touch. The occipital lobe, at the back of the head, translates the messages from the nerves in our eyes so that we can see. Beneath these lobes, the temporal lobe makes sense of sound.

> lobes: Curved divisions of the brain.
>
> inhibitions: A mental or emotional sense of restraint that holds a person back from free expression or action.

The brain's lower deck drives us to meet our biological needs so that we can survive. Its upper deck makes it possible for us to interact with and understand our world. Psychological disorders can result from disruptions of brain function in any part of the brain, but usually involve the upper deck.

How the Brain Works

Just as a computer hard drive communicates with itself and other computer parts, the brain communicates with itself and with the other parts of the body. In a single day it sends and receives billions of messages using a network of nerve cells called neurons.

Neurons consist of three structures (see Figure 2 on p. 26): dendrites, branch-like limbs protruding from the *cell body* that receive information; the cell body, the main part of a neuron and responsible for "firing" and examining messages from other neurons; and an axon, a cable-like tail that extends from the cell body and is responsible for sending messages. The end of the axon contains several terminal buttons, which overlap the dendrites of other neurons. The space between neurons is called the *synapse*. This is where nerve cells communicate with one another. Scientists estimate that the brain uses a billion neurons to send messages over a quadrillion synapses.

To send and receive messages, neurons act much like telephones (see Figure 3 on p. 27). To communicate with a friend, you pick up the phone and dial your friend's number. To initiate communication in the brain, instead of dialing a telephone, the nerve cell placing the telephone call (called a presynaptic neuron) will "fire," releasing chemicals called neurotransmitters to carry the message. Neurotransmitters, like a digital signal or telephone cable, make communication between nerve cells possible.

> terminal buttons: Found at the end of a neuron's axon, these attach to the dendrites of other neurons.
>
> neurotransmitters: Chemicals in the brain that carry messages from neuron to neuron.

The message originates in the cell body and travels through the axon. With each "firing," it is carried over the synapse by the neuron's neurotransmitters to a receiving cell called the postsynaptic neuron. But this firing doesn't mean that communication between neuron cells is complete. The chemicals need to be received by other neurons, just as your friend must pick up his phone.

Any disruption of this process (having too much of one neurotransmitter or not enough of another, blocked signals between neurons, etc.) can result in psychological disorders. Drugs used to treat mental illness primarily affect the neurotransmitters. They direct:

- how much of the neurotransmitter is sent when the sending neuron fires;

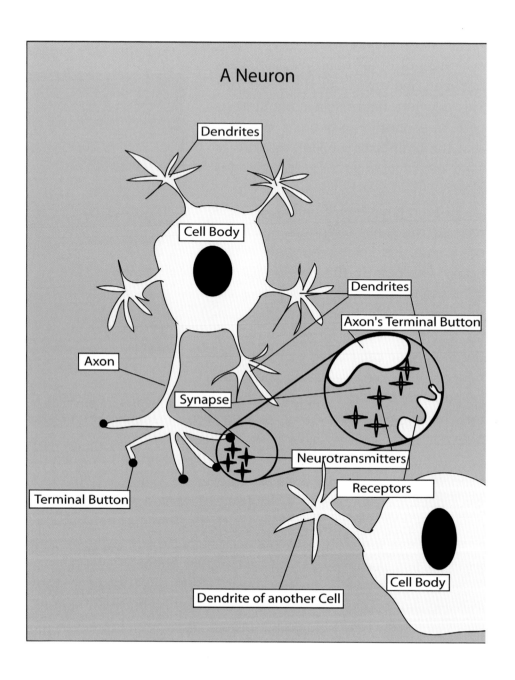

Figure 2

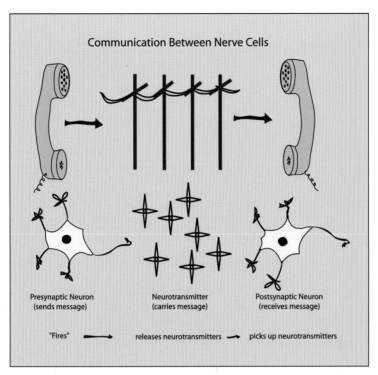

Figure 3

- how much of the neurotransmitter (if any) is received by the receiving neuron (psychiatric drugs can block their reception);
- and how much of the unused neurotransmitter is taken back by the sending cell through a process called "reuptake."

To date, scientists have identified over twenty kinds of neurotransmitters in the brain, with each being used in multiple parts of the brain. They have also found links between certain neurotransmitters and specific psychological conditions.

We think of depression as an emotion—and obsessive-compulsive disorder as a strange set of behaviors. But these disorders are actually rooted deep in the brain; scientists have linked them to the neurotransmitter serotonin. Another neurotransmitter, dopamine, can influence psychosis and attention-deficit/hyperactivity ADHD. A third chemical in the brain, gamma-aminobutyric acid (GABA), can affect anxiety disorders, drug abuse, and alcoholism.

Types of Psychiatric Drugs

The American Academy of Child and Adolescent Psychiatry groups psychiatric (or psychotropic) medication into five categories based on how they work:

- *Stimulants.* A class of medication that increases alertness, helps patients focus, and improves concentration by enhancing nerve-to-nerve communication in the brain. Common stimulants include methylphenidate hydrochloride (Ritalin), dextroamphetamine sulfate (Dexedrine), methamphetamine hydrochloride (Desoxyn), and dextroamphetamine and L-amphetamine (Adderall).

- *Antidepressants.* A type of medication generally used to help depression. Common antidepressants include fluoxetine hydrochloride (Prozac), sertraline hydrochloride (Zoloft), paroxetine hydrochloride (Paxil), amitriptyline hydrochloride (Elavil), and venlafaxine hydrochloride (Effexor).

- *Antipsychotics.* The only class of medication that can treat psychosis effectively. Some more common antipsychotics include Haloperidol (Haldol), loxapine hydrochloride (Loxitane), chlorpromazine hydrochloride (Thorazine), and clozapine (Clozaril).

- *Mood stabilizers and anticonvulsants.* A group of drugs used to stabilize emotional and behavioral swings typical of mood disorders. The most common mood stabilizer is lithium carbonate (Lithobid, Eskalith), but anticonvulsants such as carbamazepine (Tegretol) can be used to stabilize moods.

- *Antianxiety medications.* Also called *anxiolytics*, this class of medication is used to treat anxiety and panic disorders. Common anxiolytics include diphenhydramine hydrochloride (Benedryl), hydroxyzine (Vistaril), clonazepam (Klonopin), alprazolam (Xanax), lorazepam (Ativan), and diazepam (Valium).

When doctors suspect a psychological disorder, they make a diagnosis based on the criteria listed in the *Diagnostic and Statistical Manual of Mental Disorders*, and then prescribe a special class of drugs called psychiatric drugs that influence the specific chemical balance or neuron action causing the disorder. These drugs, also called psychotropics, are medications that impact brain chemistry, especially neurotransmitters. These are the kinds of drugs that ultimately helped Sarah stop obsessing about twenty-ones and helped Jeremy overcome his depression.

Psychiatric drugs seem like a miracle cure for some psychological disorders. For others, they cannot cure the disorder, but they can help its symptoms. For many patients, drug treatment alone doesn't work but needs to be used together with therapies that don't use drugs, like behavioral therapy or counseling.

Whether used alone or in conjunction with other drug or non-drug therapies, all psychiatric drugs pose certain risks. Because their effect on neurotransmitters can influence how you think, feel, and act, these drugs need to be prescribed and monitored closely by a licensed practitioner. The drug itself also needs to be safe for taking as prescribed.

Psychiatric Disorders and the Neurotransmitters That Impact Them

Psychological Disorder	Neurotransmitters
Anxiety and Phobias	GABA, Dopamine
Attention-Deficit/Hyper-activity Disorder (ADHD)	Dopamine, Norepinephrine
Depression	Serotonin, Norepinephrine, Dopamine
Insomnia (sleep disorders)	Serotonin
Obsessive-Compulsive Disorder (OCD)	Serotonin
Psychosis (includes hallucinations or delusions related to disorders such as schizophrenia)	Dopamine, Serotonin
Tic Disorders	Dopamine, Serotonin

Doctors will prescribe a psychiatric medication that is known to impact the specific neurotransmitter that is associated with the disorder.

By the 1950s, scientists had developed the first psychiatric medicines.

How do you know a pill is safe? What safeguards do we have to make sure your medication won't harm you? Have medicines always been safe? In the next chapter we'll look at the good and bad of medicinal history and how we came to have the drug manufacturing safety regulations we have today.

The manufacturers of Radithor claimed it was "harmless in every way." The medicine contained radium, however, and its side effects were extreme!

Chapter Two

Why We Need the FDA: A Brief History of Medicines in America

When did you last reach into your medicine cabinet? Did you have a headache and need some aspirin? Did you think an anti-inflammatory would help with muscle soreness or leg pain? Did sneezing and sniffling send you in search of an antihistamine? Whatever your reason for taking medication, you probably felt confident that

anti-inflammatory: A medicine that counteracts inflammation of body tissues.

antihistamine: Medication used for treating allergic reactions, especially hay fever.

Some Early Patent Medicines and Their Claims

Lydia Pinkham's Vegetable Compound, a brew of herbs and alcohol, claimed to treat menstrual cramps and cure other women's ills.

Hamlin's Wizard Oil Company's cure-all, *The Great Medical Wonder*, promised to cure headaches within five minutes, earaches in ten, and nerve disorders in fifteen. Its advertisements read, "There is no Sore it will Not Heal, No Pain it will not subdue."

Dr. Williams' Pink Pills for Pale People was advertised to be a "safe and effective tonic for the blood and nerves." Its label claimed that the pills treated anemic conditions, nervous disorders, and conditions caused by thin blood.

what you were about to take was safe, that it was, indeed, what the package said it was, and that it would do what the manufacturer said it would do.

How would you feel if you took an aspirin, only to discover that it wasn't aspirin at all but compacted chalk dust? What if you swallowed an allergy pill—and learned that it not only didn't help but made your allergies worse? Imagine what it would be like to take a liquid antibiotic only to discover that it was antifreeze for your car. You don't have to imagine. Something like that actually did happen.

In the 1930s, a pharmaceutical company named S. E. Massengill produced a medication that proved helpful in fighting bacterial infections. The medication was called "sulfanilamide." Sulfanilamide, in pill form, tasted terrible and was difficult to swallow, so the manufacturer decided to produce the same medication in liquid form.

In 1937, Massengill developed a liquid sulfanilamide solution, added some pink food coloring and cherry flavoring, and began sell-

More patent medicine "cures":

- Dunbar's Diarrhea Mixture
- Kickapoo Liver and Kidney Renovator
- Atwood's Jaundice Bitters
- Burdock Blood Bitters
- Brewer's Lung Restorer

ing the product to the public. Because of its bright color and appealing taste, the new medicine, now called "Elixir Sulfanilamide," was especially useful for children. Parents bought the tasty solution for sons and daughters who had earaches, chest colds, sore throats, high fevers—anything caused by a bacterial infection. The pill form worked well; surely the liquid form of the same medication would work well, too. Or so they thought. These parents, and the public, were in for a shocking, heartbreaking surprise.

Children treated with the new liquid didn't get well. They died.

In all, 107 people died (mostly children) from taking Elixir Sulfanilamide. Why? The chemists who developed the elixir knew that sulfanilamide could not be dissolved in water so they used a different, untested liquid in which to dissolve the helpful drug. That liquid, which became the base for the new liquid medication, was called diethylene glycol. It was much like what we use in automobile antifreeze today. The liquid used to carry a beneficial drug to bacterial infections poisoned those who took it.

What happened when so many died? According to *FDA Consumer*, the chemist who developed Elixir Sulfanilamide was so distraught over the tragic deaths his medicine caused that he committed suicide. Massengill, the company who made and marketed the pink liquid, was fined $26,100 (the maximum fine legally allowed at that time), but not otherwise held liable. More important, an outraged public cried out for action, which resulted in the passage of a new law, called the Food Drug and Cosmetic Act of 1938. This new legislation required drug companies to prove that a new drug was safe before they could sell the drug to the public.

For the first time in history, medicines would have to be tested and proved safe before release. Who would examine the proof? A government agency called the United States Food and Drug Administration (the FDA).

Before the FDA: What You See May Not Be What You Get

Prior to the Food Drug and Cosmetic Act of 1938, the United States had few laws governing medicines, drug development, and drug distribution. In the late 1800s, patent medicines reigned supreme.

patent medicines:
Medicine widely used in North America during the nineteenth and twentieth centuries. They were primarily quack cures.

You've probably seen pictures of old time medicine shows where "professors" on soapboxes or platforms in carnival tents sold their miraculous, exotic "cures." These medicine men hawked everything from Foley's Honey and Tar (for coughs and colds) to Hot Springs Liver Buttons (which promised to keep "your liver all right and your bowels regular"). Salesmanship was key: make the audience believe they're sick, then sell them what will cure their ills. The audience listened and purchased these cures because the products promised "health in a bottle" during a time of limited access to good medical care.

"Feeling weak?" the salesmen would cry. "Have digestive problems? Suffer from blood disorders or nervous conditions? No need for a doctor! Just try Dr. Williams' Pink Pills for Pale People. This little pill will cure what ails you, and may even save your life! Only fifty cents a box, six boxes for $2.50."

Drug Approval in Canada

While the United States has the FDA for the approval and regulation of drugs and medical devices, Canada has a similar organization called the Therapeutic Product Directorate (TPD). The TPD is a division of Health Canada, the Canadian government department of health. The TPD regulates drugs, medical devices, disinfectants, and sanitizers with disinfectant claims. Some of the things that the TPD monitors are quality, effectiveness, and safety. Just as the FDA must approve new drugs in the United States, the TPD must approve new drugs in Canada before those drugs can enter the market.

A popular patent medicine of the 1890s, Dr. Williams' Pink-Pill cure was only one of many patent medicines sold during the late nineteenth century. According to Dr. Tina Brewster Wray, the Curator of Collections at the White River Valley Museum in Auburn, Washington, medicine merchants marketed over 100,000 brands of patent medicines between 1860 and 1900. But these "cures" were nothing new.

Patent medicines arrived in North America in the late1700s as medicines that had been produced under grants from the English king. Under these grants, which were called "patents," the king gave his official permission for the manufacturer to develop the medicine, and he promised to provide royal financial backing. Hence the name, "patent medicine." Though usually referred to as patent medicines, the actual medicines (their recipe and ingredient list) weren't patented in North America as we think of patents today; only the medicine's name and packaging were registered with the government as a trademark to protect the remedy's owner and manufacturer. The ingredient list and recipe remained secret. That was the problem.

Most patent medicine ingredients weren't medicines at all. Though they claimed to cure everything from diaper rash to diabetes, they were often nothing more than alcohol, flavorings, herbs, or narcotics mixed together and put in a colorful bottle or box with an impressive-looking label.

Some labels and advertisements made ridiculous claims, like those made by Warner's Safe Liver and Kidney Cure. This ad claimed that Warner's medicine could treat all diseases of the lower half of the body!

Another patent medicine, Wintersmith's Chill Tonic, claimed to cure malaria—a remarkable claim for the early 1890s, considering that the World Health Organization attributes more than one million deaths annually to malaria today.

Most patent medicines claimed to work miracles, but ultimately did nothing to heal people, and in some cases caused harm.

Historical newspapers and magazines recount the sensational case of Pittsburgh millionaire and industrialist Eben Byers. In 1928, Mr. Byers injured himself at a post-game party following the annual Yale-Harvard football game. On the advice of his physician, Byers drank three half-ounce bottles per day of a patent medicine called Radithor to ease his pain and overcome his injury. He continued this treatment for two years but stopped abruptly when his teeth started falling out. Though the manufacturer claimed that Radithor was "harmless in every respect," the concoction contained radium, a radioactive element, which not only caused Byers' loss of teeth but also ate away the bones of his jaw and skull. It caused his death in 1931.

According to U.S. National Library of Medicine, one of the worst results of patent medicine use in the late nineteenth and early twentieth centuries was the number of healthy babies who became addicted to morphine, heroin, opium, or alcohol. How did babies develop these addictions?

Imagine being a mother or father with an infant who won't stop crying. The baby shrieks night and day. You never get to sleep. You can't rest. You're exhausted and your child is miserable. As a parent, if you could find a cure for your baby's misery, would you buy it? Of course you would, just as thousands did at the turn of the twentieth century.

The problem was not with the parents but with the cure. Most "soothers" or "soothing syrups," as the patent medicines sold to calm crying children were called, contained morphine, heroin, opium, or other addictive narcotics. You can be sure that the drug-laced syrups made children sleep, but the children also ended up addicted to the drug the syrups contained. Because no laws required manufacturers to list ingredients on a medicine's label, parents didn't know what was in the medicines they bought.

Today, it would be like putting crack cocaine in milk, packaging it in a medicine bottle, labeling the bottle as a safe sleep aid for children, and selling it to a mother to soothe her crying baby. The child would most certainly sleep—but would end up addicted to cocaine. And the mother would never know why.

On October 7, 1905, a newspaper reporter, Samuel Hopkins Adams, published the first of a ten-week investigative report on the patent medicine industry for *Collier's Weekly*. Called "The Great American Fraud," his series of articles exposed the deceit and trickery of the patent medicine industry—how they were marketing and selling cures that weren't really cures at all. His articles also revealed the dangerous side effects of patent medicines and their inaccurate labeling. By using in his articles startling images of skulls and death superimposed over medicine bottles, Adams caught the public's attention, the public demanded action, and a new law was born.

On June 30, 1906, with the support of President Theodore Roosevelt, Congress passed the Pure Food and Drug Act of 1906. Because of this law, product labels now had to accurately list ingredients and ingredient strength. Medicine labels also had to declare the presence of narcotics, opiates, or other addictive drugs. For the first time in American history, consumers would know what they were getting in the medicines they purchased.

You might think that the Pure Food and Drug Act of 1906, which required accurate labeling, and the Food Drug and

Cosmetic Act of 1938, which required proof of safety, would have provided adequate regulation for the drug industry, but it took one more tragedy to shape our drug laws so that we can have safe, effective medicines today.

Thalidomide: Worldwide Tragedy, Narrow Miss for the United States

For exhausted men and women living in the 1950s, a new sleep aid released in Germany seemed like an easy cure. Called thalidomide, the drug claimed to provide a quick, natural slumber for those who had difficulty falling asleep at night. It was also said to help with nausea, especially morning sickness. Thalidomide's manufacturer assured patients that the drug was safe, non-addictive, and that it wouldn't cause any kind of "hangover" side effect. By 1960, millions of people with insomnia and thousands of expectant women used this medication in Germany and throughout the world.

In September 1960, a U.S. pharmaceutical company, Richardson-Merrell, submitted an application to the FDA to begin marketing this wonder drug in the United States. Because the Food Drug, and Cosmetic Act of 1938 required manufacturers to prove their drugs were safe, Richardson-Merrell had to provide proof of thalidomide's safety in their application to the FDA. The FDA assigned a new reviewer, Dr. Frances Oldham Kelsey, to look over the application. The young physician had concerns about thalidomide's safety from the start.

morning sickness: Nausea experienced by pregnant women, usually on arising.

testimonials: Expressions of appreciation for benefits received.

verifiable: Being able to determine if something is true.

Important Dates in U.S. Drug Law History

1906: *Pure Food and Drug Act.* In response to public outcry over the evils of patent medicines, Congress passed this act to protect consumers from unknown ingredients in foods and medicines. Essentially a labeling law, this legislation required food and medicine labels to accurately and completely list product ingredients.

1938: *Federal Food Drug and Cosmetic Act.* Congress passed this law in response to the Elixir Sulfanilamide tragedy. Expanding the original act of 1906 to include foods, medicines, and cosmetics, this act required all labels to be accurate and complete and to include dosage and usage information. One of this act's most important provisions required new drugs to be proven safe before they could be marketed to the public. This act gave the FDA authority to review safety documentation and to accept or deny applications for new drugs.

1962: *Kefauver-Harris Drug Amendments.* These amendments to the 1938 Federal Food Drug and Cosmetic Act required manufacturers to prove that their drug products were safe and effective in treating the conditions for which they were intended.

In an interview published by the FDA Office of Public Affairs, Dr. Kelsey recalls, "The clinical reports were more [like] testimonials, rather than the results of well-designed, well-executed studies." Though these testimonials may have provided sufficient assurance of safety for some countries, they were not considered adequate proof by the FDA. Kelsey needed more verifiable documentation before she would approve the drug for sale in the United States. Her stubbornness, though frustrating to Richardson-Merrell, spared the U.S. public what could have been another national tragedy.

The Medicine Hall of Shame and Maim

Be glad you never tried these products:

- *Radithor*. This radioactive liquid sold as a patent medicine in the late 1920s ultimately led to the user's slow and painful death from radiation poisoning.
- *Lash Lure*. A cosmetic product of the 1930s, this eyelash dye blinded many women. One Lash Lure user died, all for want of lovely eyelashes.
- *Elixir Sulfanilamide*. Touted as a more palatable version of the sulfanilamide pill, this tasty liquid antibiotic released in 1937 resulted in more than one hundred deaths. Why? The liquid in which the medicine was dissolved was basically antifreeze.
- *Thalidomide*. All its tired users wanted was sleep. All its pregnant users wanted was relief from morning sickness. Though this medicine gave patients a good night's rest and settled their stomachs, it caused ten thousand children to be born horribly disfigured. Many thalidomide babies had no arms, legs, hands, and feet; they had only "flippers" attached to their shoulders and hips.

During her review process, the young physician discovered reports of seriously handicapped children born to European, South American, and Canadian mothers who had taken thalidomide during their first three months of pregnancy. Even one thalidomide pill, taken only one time, had resulted in children born with severely deformed limbs or without legs and arms at all. Thalidomide was harming children in their mothers' wombs.

In all, the FDA estimates that over ten thousand babies in forty-six countries were born disfigured because of thalidomide use by their mothers. Because of Dr. Kelsey's vigilance, only seventeen such children were born in the United States. A headline in the July 15, 1962, issue of *The Washington Post* reads "Heroine of the FDA Keeps Bad Drug Off of Market." In so doing, she saved countless American children from harm.

The resulting publicity surrounding the thalidomide tragedy resulted in yet another set of drug regulations in the United States: the Kefauver-Harris Amendments of 1962. These amendments strengthened the laws passed in 1938 by requiring that all new drugs be not only safe (as the laws of 1938 required) but also effective for their intended use.

The amendments also increased FDA control of drug experiments on human beings and required that manufacturers send reports of any dangerous side effects or consequences to the FDA. When manufacturers sent drug advertisements to doctors, the ads were required to inform the doctors of both the benefits of the drug and its risks or possible side effects. Most doctors who prescribed thalidomide to their sleep-deprived patients had no idea that the drug could harm unborn children. Now they would know.

The FDA Today

Today's FDA is the primary consumer protection agency in the United States. Operating under the authority given it by the government, and guided by laws established throughout the twentieth century, the FDA has established a rigorous drug approval process that verifies the safety, effectiveness, and accuracy of labeling for any drug marketed in the United States.

What does that approval process look like? How is it entered? How does an idea for treatment actually become the pill you find in your medicine cabinet? The next chapter answers these and other questions as it provides an overview of today's FDA drug approval process.

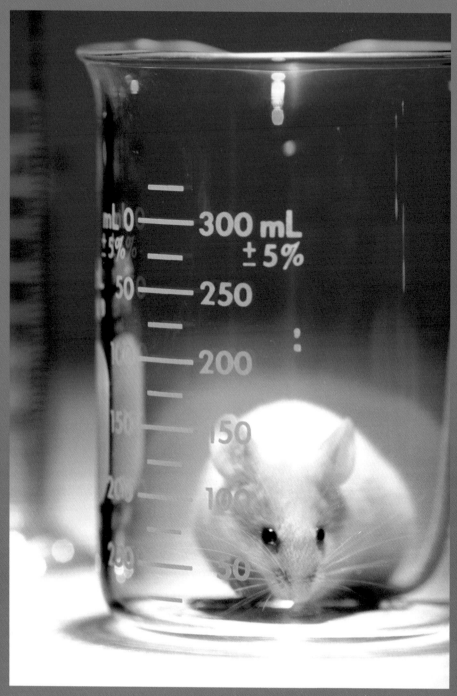

Researchers often use animals to test the safety of medications as they are developed.

Chapter Three

From Test Tube to Pill: The FDA Approval Process

I f you could spend $800 million on any one thing, what would you spend it on? If you could work on only one project for the next fifteen years, what would it be? What if you thought you had a cure for cancer? Would you spend that kind of time and money to get your cure out of the laboratory and into the public's hands?

Reports suggest that pharmaceutical companies spend, on average, anywhere from $1 billion to $12 billion to move a drug through research and development, FDA approval, and onto your pharmacist's shelves. They estimated that the process can take ten to

The FDA Approval Process: The Big Picture

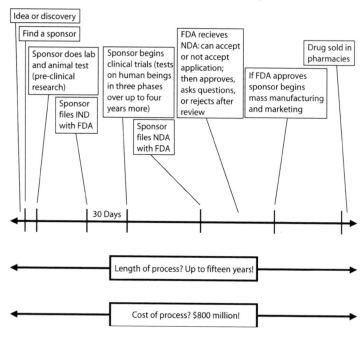

Idea or discovery

Find a sponsor

Sponsor does lab and animal test (pre-clinical research)

Sponsor begins clinical trials (tests on human beings in three phases over up to four years more)

FDA recieves NDA: can accept or not accept application; then approves, asks questions, or rejects after review

If FDA approves sponsor begins mass manufacturing and marketing

Drug sold in pharmacies

Sponsor files IND with FDA

Sponsor files NDA with FDA

30 Days

Length of process? Up to fifteen years!

Cost of process? $800 million!

fifteen years from discovery to approval by the FDA. Though medicines are discovered and developed in a variety of ways, in order to be marketed in the United States, every new drug must go through the same approval process. It is a rigorous multistage process set up by the FDA.

Start with an Idea

In a mist-filled jungle of the Amazon rain forest, Dr. Richard Campbell struggled to reproduce what he thought was the medical breakthrough of the twentieth century. After studying a local tribe for nearly six years, the aging physician learned that these people, generation after generation, year after year, never contracted cases of our modern-day plague—cancer. But why?

A local medicine man showed Dr. Campbell a brilliant pink, tubular flower that grew high above the tribal villages in the rain forest canopy. Reachable only by using a series of ropes and pulleys, the plant seemed to be the source of the cancer cure the researcher desperately sought. Locals used the flower much like American baseball players used chewing tobacco; they chewed its petals. They also put parts of the plant into all their foods. The tribal medicine man mixed the plant in many of his remedies. Since the plant grew only in the immediate region where the tribe lived, and since this was the only known human group on earth to eat this plant, and since this was also the only group of humans ever to have no history of cancer, Dr. Campbell assumed that the plant was responsible.

After observing the medicine man make his cures, Dr. Campbell used some of the native's ingredients and made his first batch of anticancer serum. Would it work?

A woman from a different tribe came to Dr. Campbell with lumps growing in her throat. The researcher sent the dying woman to the nearest medical facility—a three-day journey on foot—where

Scientists test their ideas with careful research.

medical doctors examined her. The lumps turned out to be malig-nant tumors, and they sent her home to die.

Certain he had a cure, Dr. Campbell injected the woman with his new flower extract. Overnight, in less than twenty-four hours, her tumors were gone! Just to be sure her healing wasn't a fluke, Dr. Campbell infected rats in his primitive laboratory with samples of the woman's cancerous cells the doctor had saved. The rats grew tumors. He treated them with his serum, and they all got well. Every single one.

malignant: Containing cancer cells.

With just a few samples left of his first batch of serum, the researcher tried to make more batches, but each proved worthless. None of the new batches worked on cancer-stricken rats. Here, in the jungles of South America, a cure for cancer was found and lost. That is, until something unexpected happened.

A young research assistant working with Dr. Campbell was testing a machine called a chromatograph, which is used in field research labs to analyze the contents of test samples. If, for example,

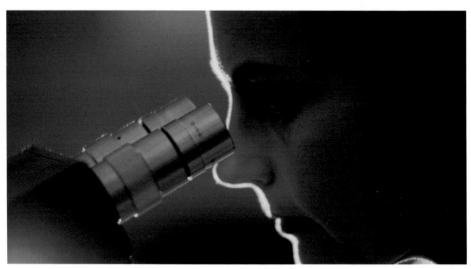

Researchers work to find treatments for the many diseases human beings encounter.

Increasing Costs of Drug Development

Studies Done by the Tufts Center for the Study of Drug Development

Year Study Completed	Dollar Value	Total Cost for Developing a New Prescription Drug
1979	Cost calculated in year 1976 dollar values	$54 million
1991	Cost calculated in year 1987 dollar values	$231 million
2002	Cost calculated in year 2000 dollar values	$802 million
2006	Cost calculated in year 2005 dollar values	$1.2 billion

you were to put dirt into the machine, it would tell you exactly what substances were contained in the dirt. If, just to be silly, you put a chocolate chip cookie into the machine, it would tell you that the cookie was made of sugar, brown sugar, eggs, butter, baking soda, vanilla, flour, salt, and chocolate chips.

The assistant had run out of the sugar-and-water solution she normally used to test the machine, but made more using local sugar and water. While the test was running, Dr. Campbell noticed that the cancer-curing product he couldn't reproduce was showing up on the

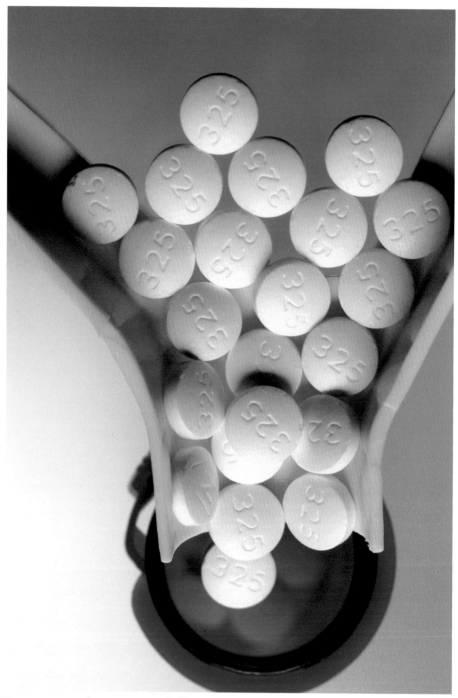

Every new drug must follow the FDA's steps for development before it can be officially approved.

machine. Where could the drug have come from? No flower petals were in the machine!

"What are you doing?" Dr. Campbell asked his assistant.

"Running a baseline," she replied.

"What are you using?" he inquired, trying to contain his excitement.

"Sugar solution."

"The same solution you've been using all along?"

"No. I ran out, so I made more."

"What did you use to make it?"

"Just some sugar I found in the sugar bowl."

In an "ah-ha!" moment, the doctor dumped out his supply of sugar and found ants—the same kind of ants that lived in the roots of the flower he thought was his miracle cure. It wasn't the flower after all. It had been the ants all along!

Did Dr. Campbell really find a cure for cancer? Unfortunately, no. Dr. Richard Campbell is the fictional research scientist played by Sean Connery in the 1992 hit *Medicine Man*. But his experience illustrates a point.

Drug manufacturers come up with ideas for new medicines and drug treatments in a variety of ways. Sometimes it's by accident, as was the case with Dr. Campbell and the accidental discovery of ants in the sugar. Sometimes a company determines to develop a new drug for a specific disorder or medical condition. Other times, research scientists change existing drug formulas or use old drugs in new ways to see if the new usages are more effective. Research or studies done by government labs, medical establishments, or universities can also prompt a drug company to develop new drugs.

No matter how a new treatment is discovered, every new drug must follow the steps for development established by the FDA before it can be approved for sale to people in the United States. That process begins with a sponsor.

A sponsor is the person, company, institution, or organization that is responsible for developing and marketing the drug. They can be, but don't have to be, the ones who discovered the drug (some-

What's Included in a New Drug Application?

NDAs can have as many as fifteen different parts and contain various amounts of information depending on the drug involved in the application. Despite these variances, every NDA must include:

- Preclinical study results (lab analysis and animal testing data)
- Clinical study results (data from tests on human beings)
- Manufacturing information (how the drug will be made)
- Labeling information (what information will be included in the package insert, on the product packaging, and on the product label)
- Patent information and certification

times sponsors buy a new drug or an idea for a new drug from the discoverer to develop it). Sponsors pay for and set up the research labs. They run tests and research experiments. They collect and study the research data. They initiate *preclinical research*.

Preclinical Research

Preclinical studies are tests done *before* ("pre") the drug is tested in human beings. These studies often include tests done on animals or in laboratory settings. Drug companies and other sponsors try to use as few animals as possible and treat these animals as humanely as possible. The FDA has established guidelines for how animal testing should be handled and what kinds of tests need to be done.

One FDA guideline mandates that a drug under development must be tested in two or more non-human species, usually one rodent (rat, mouse, etc.) and one non-rodent (monkey, rabbit, etc.).

Why? Because drugs can affect one species differently than another.

Researchers use animals, just as our fictional character Dr. Campbell used rats, to test how much of a drug can be absorbed into the blood, how quickly it is absorbed and broken down, what byproducts are created by the breakdown process, how toxic the drug is, and how quickly the body rids itself of the drug. It's important to know how different species respond to these tests in order to guess how the drug might act in human beings.

Another FDA guideline requires that preclinical studies be done over short-term (two weeks to three months) and long-term (a few weeks to several years) periods of time.

This helps researchers identify possible consequences of the drug's use that might not show up in the first few weeks of testing.

If, after collecting all this data, the preliminary research shows that a drug looks safe and promising for use in human beings, the sponsor approaches the FDA with his results. How? By filing an Investigational New Drug (IND) application.

From Studies to Store Shelves: The FDA Approval Process

An IND is not a request for permission to develop a drug; it is a report of the preclinical studies done on a drug so far and a statement of the sponsor's intent to begin testing the drug in human beings. The IND includes a complete description of the drug, its chemical structure, the drug's lab test results, its results from animal testing so far, and information on how the drug is made. The IND also includes a detailed plan describing how the sponsor intends to test the drug in humans, who will be tested, what tests will be done, how they will be done, for how long, and what risks are involved.

Once an IND is filed, the FDA has thirty days to respond, but the FDA doesn't approve or reject an IND per se. If the data contained in an IND demonstrates that enough research had been completed in

Many drugs were originally developed from natural substances.

Drugs with Weird Origins

Drug Name	Drug Origin	Drug Use
Penicillin	mold	First drug used to combat bacterial infections. It is credited with saving countless lives.
Taxotere	yew plant needles	Kills cancer cells, especially in breast and lung cancers.
Taxol	bark of Pacific yew tree	Initially a white powder, when prepared becomes a clear liquid used intravenously for chemotherapy.
Synercid	Argentinean dirt	Recently discovered, powerful antibiotic used to fight antibiotic-resistant bacterial infections. It is credited with saving the life of a high-school shooting victim who struggled with post-operative infections.

lab and animal studies to predict the drug's *probable* safe use in humans, and if the proposed plan for testing in humans is acceptable, then the FDA will do nothing and the sponsor can start testing the drug in people. FDA inaction on an IND (no reply from the FDA) only means that the sponsor can move ahead with clinical trials (tests on human beings) as they are outlined in the IND; it is not blanket approval for any kind of testing in people, nor is it approval for marketing the drug.

If the IND doesn't provide enough information, if the tests done on animals don't provide clear, positive results, or if the plan for human testing raises concern, the FDA will send a "letter of clinical hold" to the sponsor within thirty days telling them that they cannot proceed with tests in people. This letter contains specific reasons for not allowing the tests and gives the sponsor the opportunity to correct the problems or to respond to FDA objections.

If the FDA has no objections to the information contained in the IND, the sponsor can start testing the new drug in human beings. But will the drugs harm them? Will they make them sick? Could people in these tests die? Are there any laws to protect people who are willing to be "guinea pigs" for drug testing?

Protecting People Who Participate in Clinical Trials

The safety of human test subjects has not always been a primary concern for researchers. In fact, until as recently as 1974, scientists and sponsors could decide for themselves what was safe and what was not safe when they ran clinical trials. With the exception of a few guidelines established in the early 1960s, which stated that test subjects had to give informed written consent to be tested, there were few laws to govern these studies. Unfortunately, some scientists and researchers cared more about their research than they did the people in their studies, and some people were seriously harmed.

In the 1950s, researchers gave soldiers stationed at Fort Bragg, North Carolina, a new, untested drug called lysergic acid diethylamide (LSD) without telling them what it was. After being given LSD, they were expected to perform their duties as normal. Imagine driving a tank, handling a weapon, or performing other maneuvers while "high" on this highly addictive substance! Today, LSD, also called "acid," is known as a dangerous street drug that causes hallucinations and changes how your five senses perceive things (for example, LSD users claim to "hear" colors and "see" sounds). LSD can also cause terrifying experiences and nightmarish delusions. Some users, thinking they could fly, died while trying to walk out of windows or off tall buildings. This is the same drug the army tested on soldiers without their knowledge in the 1950s. These kinds of tests weren't only done at Fort Bragg. At a psychiatric institute in New York, drugs tested in patients (without knowledge or consent) killed at least one person.

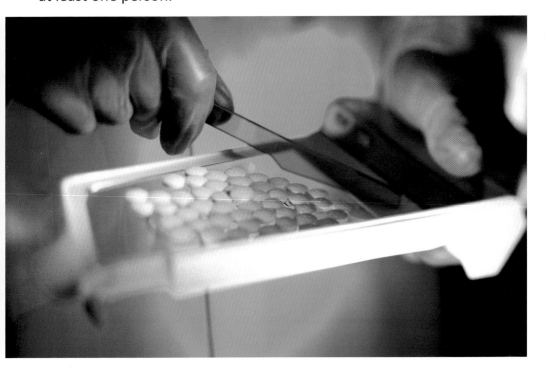

FDA experts review the work being done in pharmaceutical labs.

Another incident in which human test subjects faced grave danger occurred because doctors wanted to find a cancer cure. John Doe (not his real name) was a patient in a New York hospital in the early 1960s. Researchers trying to find a cure for cancer told John that they needed to perform a "skin test" that would measure how well his body resisted infection. That skin test, a simple injection, was actually an experiment in how live cancer cells affect the human body. The shot, which John believed was a legitimate medical test, was actually a needle loaded with live cancer cells that the doctors injected into John's body. Thankfully, John and several other patients who were given the same test did not contract cancer, and the study was stopped shortly after it started.

Other patients were less fortunate, and these patients were too young to help themselves. In the 1950s, doctors at another state institution in New York deliberately infected children with intellectual disabilities in their care with a life-threatening liver disease called hepatitis. Why? Researchers wanted to try out a new

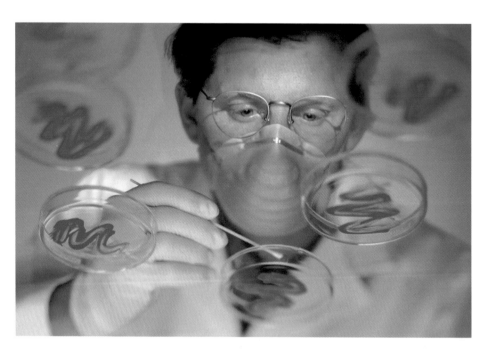

FDA experts review the work being done in pharmaceutical labs.

Too Little Too Late

"The United States government did something that was wrong—deeply, profoundly, morally wrong."
—*U.S. President Bill Clinton in May 1997, apologizing to eight survivors of the Tuskegee Syphilis Experiment.*

vaccine they hoped could treat the deadly disease. No laws prevented them from doing so.

One of the worse incidents of unethical, harmful medical testing done to human beings in U.S. history involved nearly six hundred African-American men who were observed for *forty years* by doctors at Georgia's Tuskegee Institute. Four hundred of the six hundred men had syphilis, a sexually transmitted disease that, if not treated, can lead to death. Though the study started in 1932, when there was no cure for syphilis, doctors discovered a cure for the disease in the 1950s. Instead of telling the men that they had syphilis and giving them the medicine that could save their lives, Tuskegee doctors told these men they had "bad blood" and gave them fake, worthless, sometimes painful treatments. Doctors deliberately didn't tell these men the truth because they wanted to see what the disease would do to the human body—something they could discover only after syphilis killed the men and researchers performed autopsies on their bodies. As many as one hundred of the syphilis-infected men died during the forty-year study.

> autopsies: Physical examinations of a body after death to determine cause of death.

The American public didn't know about this experiment until a national newspaper broke the story in 1972. Again, scandal and tragedy caused a public outcry, and Congress passed a new law, called the National Research Act of 1974, which protects people who participate in clinical studies. It required that all research paid for by the government be carefully reviewed by committees called institutional review boards (IRBs). The U.S. government's Department of Health and Human Services also created a new organization called the Office of Health and Human Services to oversee the IRBs.

IRBs hire full-time experts to visit research sites and facilities. These experts inspect the labs. They talk to people being used in the tests in order to make sure each participant has knowingly consented to be in the study. They talk to the researchers. They review test results. They make sure that the risks involved aren't too great. They compare research papers with what they see at research sites and with other comparable studies. The IRBs look for problems in testing methods or in how test subjects are treated. If people are being harmed, put at unnecessary risk, or aren't informed of what is happening to them, the IRBs can shut down the testing.

This law and the presence of IRBs provide enough accountability to make most research studies involving human beings today safe and ethical. Most people who participate in these tests know exactly what they're getting into. They know which tests to expect and what risks they will face. Because of the FDA's and IRBs' watchful eyes, as well as federal legislation, it is safer today to participate in clinical trials than it ever has been.

Clinical Trials: Testing New Drugs in Humans

New drugs intended to treat people need to be tested on people to demonstrate their safety and effectiveness. Unless some people are willing to be guinea pigs, no one would know about a drug's impact on human beings before it is sold to millions of unsuspecting customers. Think about it. If you were about to take a brand new medicine, one that had just been put on store shelves for the very first time, wouldn't you want to know that the drug had been used safely in other people first? But testing a new drug in people for the first time can be risky. Because so much is at stake, researchers must obtain informed consent from people they plan to use in the study before it can begin. Informed consent means that the researcher is required to:

- Provide the people being tested with enough information about the study for them to be able to make responsible choices about their involvement.
- Answer any questions the person being tested might have.
- Make sure that the person being tested understands all the risks and responsibilities that go along with being part of the study.
- Make sure the person used in the trial knows of other treatment options, especially if that person is a patient being used to test a new treatment for his illness.
- Make sure that the person to be included in the test is participating by voluntary choice (no one is making him participate against his will).

Once researchers obtain a participant's informed consent in writing, they may begin testing their new drugs in those people. These clinical trials progress slowly and carefully through three stages called Phase One, Phase Two, and Phase Three.

Phase One clinical trials happen when the drug is given to human beings for the very first time. This phase tracks the drug's effect on a small number of healthy volunteers (usually twenty to one hundred), lasts several months, and is used to determine the safety of the drug for human beings. Starting with very small doses, which are gradually increased, the sponsor closely watches each participant for signs of any unexpected side effects, unwanted reactions, or safety risks. The sponsor also tests the participants to see how

Three Phases of Tests Done on Humans (Clinical Studies)

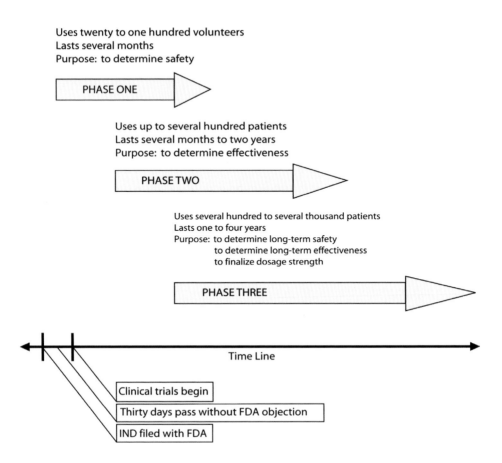

Uses twenty to one hundred volunteers
Lasts several months
Purpose: to determine safety

PHASE ONE

Uses up to several hundred patients
Lasts several months to two years
Purpose: to determine effectiveness

PHASE TWO

Uses several hundred to several thousand patients
Lasts one to four years
Purpose: to determine long-term safety
           to determine long-term effectiveness
           to finalize dosage strength

PHASE THREE

Time Line

Clinical trials begin

Thirty days pass without FDA objection

IND filed with FDA

the drug works in the body, how it is broken down, how long it stays in the body, and, if possible, whether it shows any sign of doing what it was designed to do.

Phase Two clinical studies move the drug testing from healthy volunteers to patients afflicted with the condition the new drug is designed to treat. This phase is primarily intended to reveal the drug's effectiveness (how well it works). Lasting several months to two years, Phase Two clinical trials closely monitor several hundred patients and look for short-term side effects and risks as well as the drug's ability to do what it claims.

Phase Three clinical studies, which last one to four years (or more) and use several hundred to several thousand people, begin only after earlier studies provide evidence that the drug is relatively safe and works as intended in people. This larger group study is designed to discover additional information about the drug's benefits and its risks over time. Phase Three trials also provide information on dosage (how much of the drug the patient needs to take in order for the drug to work).

These three phases don't occur one right after the other. They overlap. And though the purpose of the trials is ultimately to determine a drug's safety and effectiveness, the primary concern during clinical trials is for the safety of the people in the study. The drug sponsor must stay in constant communication with the FDA about how the studies are going, and if at any time the FDA feels the people being tested are being put in jeopardy, the FDA can stop the testing and prevent further tests from being started. This is also called a "clinical hold."

Let's assume that a sponsor's clinical trials all go well. The research goes smoothly, the drug makes it through all three phases, and it seems to work effectively and safely in human beings. Can the sponsor go out and sell its new drug to the public? Not yet.

The sponsor first has to file a New Drug Application (NDA) with the FDA. An NDA is the application a sponsor makes requesting the FDA to give approval for the sponsor to begin manufacturing and marketing a new drug to the public. It essentially asks, "Do we have your approval to make this drug and to sell it to doctors, pharmacies, and in stores?"

NDA: A Formal Request for FDA Approval

Since the federal Food Drug and Cosmetic Act passed in 1938, every new drug sold in the United States has been required to have an NDA approved by the FDA before the drug can be sold to the public. The NDA provides the "proof" the FDA needs to ensure that

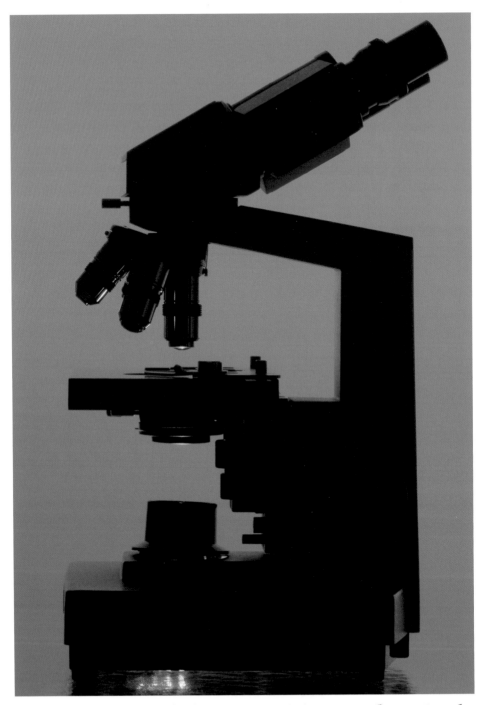

Researchers may use high-power microscopes to determine the effects of various chemicals on living tissue.

the drug won't harm most people and will actually work when used as prescribed. To demonstrate that proof, the application has to include animal and human testing results, clinical data from human drug trials (including case studies), the drug's chemical and physical makeup, details on how the drug will be manufactured, what form the drug will take (pill, capsule, liquid, etc.), what kind of packaging will be used for the drug, and what the labeling will say. Test results in the NDA must show that the drug is both safe and effective—in other words, it can't unduly harm people, and it must work.

When the FDA receives an NDA from a sponsor, several different things can happen:

- The FDA can look at the overall application and decide that the application isn't complete enough to bother reviewing. All required parts of the application are not there, so the FDA won't even begin a review. The application is considered unacceptable.
- The FDA can look at the application, see that most required parts are there, and declare that the application can be reviewed, but that they still need more information.
- The FDA can look at the application, see that all the required parts are there, and begin to review each part of the application.

Once the review process begins, again several things can happen.

- The FDA can review each part of the application and decide they need clarification on certain parts. The FDA will go back to the sponsor with specific questions about those parts of the application. The sponsor then has to answer those questions satisfactorily before the application can be approved. This is what happens with almost every new drug application filed with the FDA.
- In very rare instances, the FDA will review each part of the application, decide that the application is in order, and approve the drug for sale to the public.

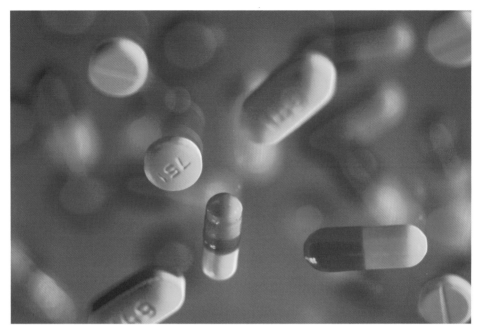

The FDA does its best to ensure that each pill we take is safe.

- Also in very rare instances, the FDA will reject the findings of an NDA and reject approval for a drug. Why is this rare? Because most drugs that need to be rejected because of safety or ineffectiveness are weeded out during clinical trials. Their development process never makes it this far.
- In other rare instances, the FDA will review an application and decide that a drug is too important (as in being a possible cure for a deadly disease) to withhold approval for, even though the research data isn't completely clear about its safety and effectiveness. A recent illustration of this kind of accelerated approval involves experimental drug treatments used for HIV.

Let's say that the sponsor dots all of his "i's" and crosses all of his "t's"—he answers all of the FDA's questions, everything is in order, and the drug is approved. The sponsor begins making the drug, packaging it, and distributing it all over the country. You see the drug advertised on TV and sold in your local drug store. Is that the end of the story? Is the FDA out of the picture once a drug is approved?

No. The FDA has provisions for something called Phase Four studies and post-marketing surveillance. We look at these important safeguards in the next chapter.

HIV: Human immunodeficiency virus, a virus that attacks the human immune system and often leads eventually to AIDS.

An adolescent who is "hyperactive" may have a psychiatric disorder—and medication may offer him help.

Chapter Four

After Approval: Are Psychiatric Drugs Safe?

Twelve-year-old Kevin couldn't sit still. He fidgeted constantly. His teacher considered him "immature" for his age (just as all his previous teachers had). He found it difficult to pay attention and nearly impossible to stay organized. He sometimes did things without thinking, which got him into trouble, and though he worked hard, he didn't do well in class. He had trouble making and keeping friends at school. His father thought he was lazy and yelled at him when he forgot assignments or didn't do what he was told to do. His mother worried about him and called the doctor.

How Can I Report an Adverse Reaction?

If you or someone you are with has an adverse reaction, call your doctor immediately. FDA guidelines for reporting adverse reactions suggest that you:

1. Report what happened as soon as possible. Be specific and complete in your description about what the adverse reaction was and how it affected you or the person you were with (if that person had the reaction).
2. Give the name, address, and phone number of the person affected.
3. When reporting for someone else, include your name, address, and phone number.
4. If you or your friend had to go to the hospital to receive treatment for the adverse reaction (for example, if you had a severe allergic reaction and needed to go to the emergency room), make sure to give the name of the doctor or hospital where treatment was provided.
5. Give a complete description of the product causing the adverse reaction (brand name, chemical name, dosage, code numbers or lot numbers on its packaging, where you purchased it, date of purchase, etc.).

After several tests and evaluations, Kevin learned that he had ADHD. His doctor recommended that he start on five milligrams of Ritalin (methylphenidate) daily to help his concentration. Kevin felt relieved when he learned that his inability to pay attention and difficulty focusing had a name and a cause. He was even more relieved that a small round white pill could help.

The change in Kevin was as immediate as it was obvious. Almost overnight he seemed able to sit still and listen to his teachers. Two days after starting his medication he noticed that he didn't forget as much as he had before. He was less impulsive and far more able to concentrate. He even started completing assignments and finishing tasks on his own. Kevin began to feel good about himself, perhaps for the very first time.

Then the tics started.

A few days into treatment, while playing a video game, Kevin started smacking his lips and swallowing a lot. That progressed to his unconsciously sniffing and clearing his throat. He didn't notice at first, but his mother did. She called the doctor.

nightcaps: An alcoholic drink taken at the end of the day.

"It is probably a side effect of the Ritalin," his doctor soothed. "It's nothing to worry about. Kevin has only been on Ritalin for a few days, and there's no history of tic disorders in the family. Let's give it a few more days to see how he adjusts. I'm sure the tics will pass."

But they didn't. Kevin's tics grew more frequent, and they started to scare him. Worse yet, kids at school made fun of his strange behavior. By the end of the week, it was clear that Kevin would need to stop taking Ritalin.

This FDA-approved drug resulted in an unexpected consequence. Though Ritalin helped Kevin as it was designed to do, it triggered a tic disorder, which disappeared shortly after Kevin discontinued his medication.

Suzanne was less fortunate.

After weeks of being unable to sleep, forty-three-year-old Suzanne had had enough. Exhausted and desperate, she called her family physician and asked him for some kind of medication that would help her sleep. He prescribed Ambien (zolpidem).

About thirty minutes before bedtime that night, Suzanne took her prescribed ten-milligram dose; ignoring the warning label on the prescription bottle, she also decided to down a few nightcaps for good measure. What could it hurt? Surely the combination of a few relaxing drinks and medication would finally put her to sleep.

It did. Permanently.

Brand Names vs. Generic Names

Talking about psychiatric drugs can be confusing, because every drug has at least two names: its "generic name" and the "brand name" that the pharmaceutical company uses to market the drug. Generic names come from the drugs' chemical structure, while drug companies use brand names to inspire public recognition and loyalty for their products.

Here are the brand names and generic names for some common psychiatric drugs:

Ativan®	lorazepam
Haldol®	haloperidol
Klonopin®	clonazepam
Paxil®	paroxetine hydrochloride
Prozac®	fluoxetine hyrdrochloride
Valium®	diazepam
Xanax®	alprazolam
Zoloft®	sertraline hydrochloride

The combination of alcohol and zolpidem caused Suzanne to stop breathing. She never woke up.

Was zolpidem safe? *Yes, when used according to prescribed guidelines.* But Suzanne opted to ignore those guidelines and paid the ultimate price.

How Safe Is Safe?

When the FDA approves a drug, as it did Kevin's Ritalin and Suzanne's Ambien, it is saying that the drug is safe and effective for public use when used as instructed. But "safe" may not mean what you think it does. What does safe really mean when referring to FDA-approved drugs?

"Safe does not mean harmless," stated Janet Woodcock, M.D., former director of the FDA's Center for Drug Evaluation and Research (CDER) in a recent interview with *FDA Consumer* magazine. "Every drug comes with risks, and our tolerance for risk is higher for drugs that treat serious and life-threatening illnesses. There is no question that cancer drugs can be highly toxic. But they also save lives."

The word safe, when applied to FDA-approved drugs, means only that the drug's effectiveness for its intended use (how well it works on the targeted disease or disorder) outweighs its risks (possible side effects). Generally speaking, if clinical studies show that a drug works and its side effects are tolerable, the drug will most likely be approved. If the drug works but kills or seriously harms the patients taking it, the drug will most likely not be approved. The risk of taking the drug has to be worth the benefit the drug provides. And that's the case for most drugs on the market.

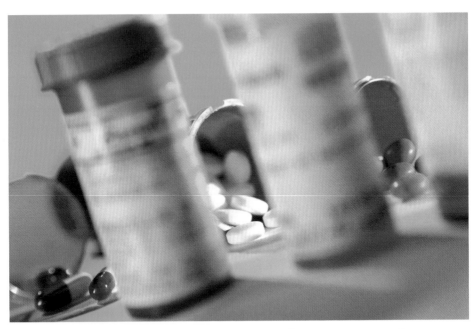

When a drug is determined to be "safe" by the FDA, that means the drug's effectiveness for its intended use outweighs its possible side effects.

What can I do to reduce the risks of taking psychiatric medicines?

1. See your doctor. Talk with him. Ask questions.
2. Be clear and complete when you describe your symptoms.
3. Tell your doctor about any medications, vitamins, herbs, or over-the-counter drugs you are currently taking.
4. Follow your doctor's directions. Take prescribed medication exactly as your doctor tells you. Don't skip or double up on doses.
5. Heed warnings on the prescription bottle or package insert.
6. Know the trade name *and* the chemical name of the drug.
7. When you start taking a new medicine, write down what you take, how much you take, when you take it, and any side effects you notice (no matter how small). This written record can provide important information for your doctor.
8. Report adverse reactions immediately, even if they seem minor.
9. Be informed! Learn as much as you can about your disorder and the medication you are taking. Look up your drug in the *Physician's Desk Reference*. If you have questions, ask your doctor.
10. Be willing to change treatment strategies if you experience adverse reactions.

Even Safe Drugs Can Cause Adverse Reactions

Before approving a drug, the FDA tries to find out about the drug's potential risks. Many side effects show up in the manufacturer's pre-approval clinical studies and are noted in the application made to the FDA. But what if a particular reaction happens in only one out of twenty-five thousand people? Or in one out of fifty thousand? Most clinical trials test drugs on only a few hundred to several thousand people. A serious reaction that occurs once in twenty-five thousand times or once in fifty thousand may be missed in these studies. That side effect might remain unknown until the drug has been used by tens or hundreds of thousands of people—a number far greater than the average number of people involved in clinical trials.

Though they endeavor to do so, the FDA and drug manufacturers can't anticipate every possible side effect of a drug in every person. Even the safest drugs, when used appropriately, can cause adverse reactions.

An adverse reaction is an unintended, unwanted side effect. It can be unpleasant or harmful, or it may just be unexpected. You can have adverse reactions to many different things: for instance, drugs, medical devices, vaccines, cosmetics, herbs, vitamins, and food, and

Not every real-life situation can be anticipated in the laboratory, so rare side effects may not be discovered until a drug has been used by many people.

these reactions can range from the mildly irritating to life threatening. Common mild adverse reactions to drugs include stomach
upset, drowsiness, dizziness, restlessness, difficulty sleeping, headache, rash, abdominal pain, and diarrhea. Kevin's tic disorder and
Suzanne's breathing difficulty and death
were severe adverse reactions.

New drugs and old drugs alike can
cause adverse reactions. Over-the-
counter antihistamines (like Benedryl),
for example, do a great job combat-
ing allergies but can cause extreme
drowsiness (not a big deal unless you
are driving a car or operating dangerous machinery—and then drowsiness
can cause serious accidents). Some
antibiotics, like penicillin, which have
been around for decades, battle bacterial infections well, but can cause mild-
to-life-threatening allergic reactions.
Other antibiotics, like tetracycline, help
people who can't take penicillin, but often cause stomach or in-
testinal discomfort. Even common household aspirin can irritate
your stomach lining. Worse yet, aspirin has been known to trigger
Reye's Syndrome when given to children battling chicken pox, influenza, or other viral infections.

Over-the-counter:
Available at a drug
store without a pre-
scription.

Reye's Syndrome: A
severe reaction in
children being given
aspirin to treat chicken
pox, influenza, and
other viral infections.

All these side effects are considered adverse reactions, whether
mild or severe, and most were observed in clinical trials before the
FDA approved each drug. The FDA weighed the drug's effectiveness
and its potential to do good against its potential to do harm, and
each was approved for public use. As CDER's Dr. Woodcock stated,
however, approval doesn't mean that the drugs are harmless—they
still might cause adverse reactions.

To make sure that prescribing physicians and the public know
about potential adverse reactions, the FDA requires manufacturers
to tell them of both the benefits *and the risks* of any new drug they

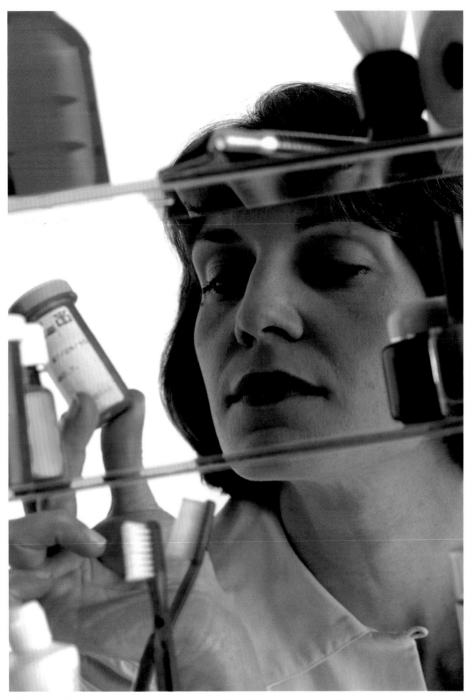

Although no system is perfect, the FDA's work allows us all to take medicines without having to worry about unforeseen reactions.

want to sell. Most doctors today know about potential adverse reactions. How are they informed?

Getting the Word Out On Medications: Package Inserts and the PDR

The FDA requires manufacturers to put together a complete report on every drug product they want to sell. This report, called a package insert, is printed on paper and put into every product's package. The FDA doesn't write these; the manufacturer does, but the FDA must approve their contents.

Have you ever noticed the tightly folded, double-sided, long, rectangular piece of paper with tiny print stuffed inside the medicine package you buy at the store? That piece of paper is the package insert, and it contains everything you need to know about that medication, good and bad. FDA guidelines require that every package insert include:

- A brief description of the drug and its intended use.
- The drug's chemical structure and form.
- The drug's "clinical pharmacology" (the way the drug works in humans and animals, how it is absorbed, how long it stays in the body, how quickly the body breaks it down, how efficiently the body uses the drug, how quickly the body gets rid of it) based on clinical trials and lab test results.
- A listing of all recorded adverse reactions and side effects to the drug.
- The drug's potential for abuse.
- Possible drug interactions (how this drug interacts with other drugs).

Common Adverse Reactions to Psychiatric Drugs

Disorder	Common Drugs Used to Treat the Disorder	Common Adverse Reactions
Depression	Prozac, Zoloft, Elavil	Dry mouth, fatigue, decreased appetite, nausea, diarrhea, headache
Attention-Deficit/ Hyperactivity Disorder (ADHD)	Ritalin	Headaches, dry mouth, decreased appetite, tremor, insomnia
Obsessive-Compulsive Disorder (OCD)	Luvox	Anxiety, decreased appetite, dizziness, dry mouth, fatigue, headache, insomnia, rash, nausea
Insomnia (Inability to Sleep)	Xanax	Drowsiness, memory impairment, poor muscle coordination
Schizophrenia	Risperdal	Anxiety, dizziness, sleepiness, nausea, constipation, rash
Bipolar Disorder and Mood Swings	Lithonate, Lithotabs	Diarrhea, increased appetite, increased thirst, tremor, weight gain

Despite their risks, psychotropic medications have an important place in health care. They can improve and save lives when prescribed appropriately. However, they should only be used when needed and taken exactly as directed by the prescribing practitioner. Misuse of both prescribed, over-the-counter, and illegal drugs can result in serious danger to a person. Patients who are prescribed medications need to understand risks, benefits and alternatives to treatment before they begin their medication—and they should never take any other drug or medicine without first checking with their practitioner.

- "Indications and usage" (which disorders the drug is intended to treat, in what situations the drug should not be used, warnings, precautions, etc.).
- Information on symptoms of drug overdose and how to counteract an overdose.
- Special instructions on what doctors should tell patients before beginning treatment.
- Dosage and administration (how to start the drug, how much to take, how to use it in special circumstances, how to safely reduce or stop the medication).
- In what form the drug is supplied (capsules, liquid, tablets, dosage strength, etc.).
- How to properly store the drug (ideal temperature, light, kind of container).

While this information equips doctors to know how and when to use these drugs, saving all those individual package inserts would be inconvenient at best. Doctors would find it difficult, if not impossible, to consult papers found in product packages every time they considered prescribing a medication. To make it easier for doctors to look up this needed information on specific drugs, one publisher compiles package insert information in an annual reference book called the *Physician's Desk Reference* (PDR). Drug manufacturers pay this publisher to include copies of their package inserts in the PDR each year for every drug they want listed. The PDR is essentially a collection of package inserts. By being listed in the PDR, each report makes it more likely that a doctor will consider that drug for use in treating patients.

The PDR provides a win-win situation. Doctors can conveniently obtain the information they need to safely prescribe medications for their patients; manufacturers can get information about their drugs into doctors' hands, which results in more sales.

One added benefit of the PDR: it is also a valuable resource for patients or other consumers who might purchase or use the drugs listed there. If Suzanne, before taking her sleep aid, had bothered to read about her medication in the PDR (which is available in public libraries and local book stores), she would have seen that Ambien and alcohol taken simultaneously could result in death. Checking the PDR (or reading the package insert) might have saved her life.

Adverse Reactions
and How to Report Them

What if you do everything right? What if you go to your doctor, discuss treatment plans, decide on the right treatment plan for you, pick up your prescribed medication, read the package insert, and follow the directions exactly as you should—will that make you immune to bad reactions to the medication? Unfortunately, no.

Twelve-year-old Gene obsessed about neatness. He arranged his closet perfectly: he hung every hanger exactly one inch from the next; he lined up his shoes with their laces tucked inside with only the soles of each pair touching; he stacked the magazines he stored on his closet shelf so that their edges lined up with the shelf edge; and if his closet's brass doorknob had a fingerprint smudge,

A person with obsessive-compulsive disorder may be constantly preoccupied with maintaining a rigid schedule. Medication can help.

he would immediately get a paper towel and some brass cleaner and polish the handle so it shined. It was the same for the mirrors in Gene's bedroom and bathroom, for his windows, and for the surface of his desk—Gene couldn't stand to see dirt smudges anywhere.

When Gene's obsession started keeping him from getting to the dinner table on time or kept him from catching the bus, his parents knew it was time to get Gene some help. They took him to a psychiatrist who diagnosed him as having obsessive compulsive disorder OCD. The psychiatrist decided that the best treatment plan for Gene would be a combination of behavior therapy and medication. She prescribed the psychiatric drug, Anafranil (clomipramine).

Gene did exactly what he was told to do. He started taking twenty-five milligrams of Anafranil every night at bedtime, and after two weeks, he noticed a difference. Smudges didn't bother him so much anymore, and he didn't feel like his closet had to be quite so perfect. But he also noticed something else. He started getting headaches; he felt dizzy a lot, especially when he first got up in the morning; and his mouth seemed dry all the time.

Though he was doing all the right things, Gene still experienced adverse reactions. Unlike Kevin's Ritalin-induced tic disorder and Suzanne's death, Gene's experience was common, and his headaches, dizziness, and dry mouth passed after his body got used to the medication.

behavior therapy: A type of non-drug treatment strategy that psychiatrists, psychologists, and counselors use to help patients overcome psychological disorders. This therapy focuses on helping the patient change his behavior by changing his thinking about the behavior, providing assignments designed to help the patient change the behavior, equipping the patient with the ability to make different behavioral choices, and providing planning strategies for changing the behavior.

The FDA requires that a drug's long-term safety statistics must be recorded and reported.

What should you do if something like this happens to you? The first and most important thing is to tell your parents (if you are a minor) and your doctor. Adverse reactions can be life threatening if not taken seriously. Only your doctor can tell which adverse reactions are potentially serious and which are not. Your doctor needs to know.

Your doctor will report any serious adverse reactions to the manufacturer and the FDA. The FDA requires that drug manufacturers keep a record of and report all known incidences of adverse reactions. If the adverse event is serious or life threatening, doctors and manufacturers must report it immediately. Minor reactions can be reported periodically, anywhere from every three to every twelve months. These reports enable the FDA to track the safety record of a drug after it has been approved and to stop the sale of a drug if serious side effects are later discovered.

Reports can come from three places:

1. the consumer or patient taking the drug;
2. the physician, pharmacist, nurse practitioner, or other health-care professional who prescribed or dispensed the drug or treated the patient's adverse reaction; and
3. the sponsor or manufacturer (the company who made and sold the drug).

When a doctor or patient tells the FDA about an adverse reaction, the report usually describes an adverse reaction that happened when the patient took the drug as part of the treatment the doctor prescribed. When the sponsor makes the report, the report can describe adverse reactions reported to the sponsor by the doctor or patient, or it can describe results from Phase Four clinical trials.

Phase Four Clinical Trials

The first three phases of clinical trials only last up to four years. Sometimes adverse reactions take a long time to develop; they can take five years or more.

To keep track of the long-term safety of a drug, the sponsor follows test subjects even after the FDA gives approval for the drug to be sold publicly. These studies can take several more years and are happening while the drug is being sold. All results from post-approval studies are reported to the FDA, too, just to ensure the long-term safety of a drug's use.

From a drug's discovery to its distribution to patients (even after approval), the FDA plays a critical role in the ongoing monitoring of a drug's safety record. It does so to keep you, the consumer, safe and informed.

Many people today are turning to "natural remedies" for their ailments.

Chapter Five

Beyond the FDA: Alternative Treatments and Medicines

She was extremely beautiful, but vain and proud, and all she wanted was to live forever. A "magic pill" would grant her wish. . . .

During the years King Yao reigned in China (around 2100 BCE), it is said that ten suns appeared in the sky, creating massive, widespread drought. The heat from so many suns scorched the land, withered the crops, and caused temperatures to rise to life-threatening levels. What could be done to save the earth and its people?

The Chinese have a long history of natural medicine.

King Yao knew of an excellent archer who served him faithfully, not only in battle but by shooting game for feasts and festivals. Houyi, the archer, was known to take down massive beasts with only one shot. He possessed the greatest archery skills in the land.

"Bring me my royal archer," the Chinese King ordered. The King's men summoned Houyi, and the young hunter approached the throne.

"Houyi," the King said fondly. "You have served me well these last years. You are the greatest archer in all the land. I fear I have nowhere else to turn."

Drawing the bowman to his side and leading him to the window, the King continued, "Do you see these ten suns? They will destroy our world and all that is in it. I need you, young friend, to shoot down nine of the ten suns. It is my command."

Swallowing his fear and wiping the sweat from his brow, Houyi nodded solemnly. "As you wish, my lord."

Drawing a single reed from his quiver, Houyi loaded the arrow onto his bow. Straightening his left arm, he hooked his right fingertips around the bowstring and drew the loaded arrow to his ear. The young archer looked down the arrow's shaft, aimed, and uncurled his fingers. His release was smooth and sure. The arrow's flight was straight and true. The first sun fell when Houyi's arrow struck its center, as did each of the eight remaining suns.

As a reward for his heroic deed, King Yao offered Houyi anything he wished. What the young archer wanted more than anything was the king's daughter's hand in marriage. Houyi had loved the princess from afar, ever since they were children. He never dreamed she could be his. Now she would be his. The peasant archer and Princess Chang'e were married.

But all was not well. The princess had been extraordinarily beautiful from the time she was very young, and she knew it. She viewed herself as the most beautiful woman in the land. Though her new husband loved her deeply and treated her like the royalty she was, she despised him and treated him with cool indifference. He was beneath her. No mere mortal was worthy of her love and respect.

How Can You Stay Motivated to Exercise?

The Mayo Clinic's 2001 release, Mayo Clinic on Depression, suggests five ways to keep up your interest in and motivation to exercise.

1. Make it fun.
2. Set goals.
3. Be flexible.
4. Spend time with others who are physically active.
5. Reward yourself.

She was, after all, the fairest maiden in the world—a world that her father feared might be destroyed.

Though pleased with the marriage, King Yao worried that the suns would return. To enable Houyi to live forever, and to forever protect the Earth from returning suns, the king gave Houyi a "magic pill"—the only one of its kind in all the land. Swallowing the pill would make Houyi immortal; he could forever protect the world from too many suns.

When Houyi's wife, Princess Chang'e learned of this incredible gift, jealousy and rage consumed her.

"Surely only someone like me," the princess muttered to herself, "only someone of divine beauty and elegance, only someone of supreme importance, deserves to live forever. Not this peasant archer who calls himself my husband! I have to have that pill!"

Late one evening, while her loyal husband slept, the princess stole Houyi's magic pill and swallowed it. Now the proud beauty's life would never end! But Princess Chang'e's immortality turned out quite differently than she expected.

Because of her foolish vanity and hateful pride, Princess Chang'e, the most beautiful woman in the world, was turned into a toad and banished to the moon for eternity.

It is said that if you look at the moon, even today, you can still see the princess sitting there, pestle in hand, trying to grind out a new magic pill.

The idea of a magic pill has been around for centuries. Magic pills are the stuff of fairy tales and folklore. We hear about magic pills in ancient legends like that of Princess Chang'e. We hear of them in stories passed from generation to generation and in advertisements for products that claimed to be cures. Nineteenth-century patent

There is no such thing as a magic pill!

medicines claimed that their magic pills could cure just about every imaginable ill. Even today we hear about magic pills that promise to do everything from make you lose weight without diets or exercise to miraculously cure deadly disease.

Myths About Psychiatric Drugs

Which of the following statements do you think is true?

- Medications are drugs, and all drugs are bad.
- Psychiatric medications are okay for adults but unsafe for kids.
- Doctors, teachers, and parents use drugs to control children, not to help them.
- Once you start on a psychiatric drug you'll never be able to stop.
- If a teen really wants to change, he or she should be able to do it without medication.
- Medication turns patients into someone they are not.
- People who need medication are weak.
- Taking medication is something to be ashamed of.
- Psychiatric medication either makes you high or turns you into a "zombie."
- Only weird or crazy people need psychiatric medication.
- Taking psychiatric drugs leads to drug addiction and abuse.

The Pennsylvania Department of Public Welfare's Office of Mental Health identifies these and other statements as myths and misconceptions about psychiatric drugs and their use. *Every one of the above statements is false.*

The truth, however, is that there is no such thing as a magic pill—even when it comes to psychiatric drugs.

Yes, psychiatric drugs seem like miracle cures because they have helped so many patients' psychological disorders. And yes, today's FDA-approved drugs are safer than any medicines in history. But ultimately, no pill can do it all. The most effective treatment for psychological disorders combines a variety of treatment options. Medication is only one option available. There are several more.

Alternatives to Psychiatric Drug Treatment

Thirteen-year-old Beth's clothes had finally gotten too tight to wear. Worse yet, her recent weight gain left her feeling tired and irritable all the time. She didn't seem to fit in anywhere anymore—not at home, not at school, not in her church youth group. She wasn't good at sports, she didn't have any real friends, and her grades, once the best in the class, were dropping.

Beth wasn't happy. She tried journaling, but her writing sessions seemed to focus too much on how miserable she felt and how tired she was. That only made her feel worse. So she tried dieting. Maybe losing weight would help her feel better about herself and give her more energy. But she gave up on that, too. It was just too hard. When her father gently probed about what was bothering her, she blew up. Her parents, once her friends and confidants, now irritated her.

Beth's father, convinced that his daughter might need help, took her to the doctor. Their family physician did a physical exam, took some blood samples, and asked a ton of questions. His preliminary diagnosis? He felt Beth was suffering from a mild form of depression.

"What can I do to get better?" Beth asked.

"Well, I could prescribe an antidepressant that seems to work well in teens."

As a health food fanatic for the last year, Beth was uneasy.

"Do I have to take drugs?"

"I don't think your symptoms warrant starting there, if you're uncomfortable with trying drug treatment. There are other things we can try first."

"Like what?" she responded skeptically.

Her doctor gave her a small smile and asked, "How much exercise are you getting?"

Beth shrugged her shoulders and looked sheepish. She had to admit she never moved unless she had to. She even found reasons to miss gym class whenever she could.

Regular Exercise

Exercise is important for anyone who wants to stay healthy, but for those suffering with certain psychological disorders, exercise can provide great benefits! Exercise influences the neurotransmitters in your brain in much the same way as antidepressant medication. It can help you sleep better at night and feel more energetic during the day. It can also help you feel better about yourself.

How can you safely start an exercise program?

- Consult your family doctor to make sure you don't have any health conditions that could prevent you from exercising safely.
- Pick an exercise you enjoy. What is fun for you? Swimming? Bicycling? Walking? Jogging? Tennis? Weight lifting? Aerobics? If you enjoy an exercise activity, you are more likely to stick with it.
- Start small. Don't expect too much from yourself too soon. Shoot for fifteen minutes of exercise three days a week to start. Then gradually increase your time and number of days

Regular exercise is an important component of good health.

per week as your body gets used to being active again. Always give yourself at least one day off.

- Take it outside. Fitness experts say that exercising outdoors can improve your outlook as well as your performance.
- Buddy up. Exercise with someone. That can mean anything from joining a team sport to finding a walking partner. Having someone to exercise with improves your chances of showing up on days when you'd rather stay home.

Citrus fruits supply Vitamin C, essential to good health.

These are just a few tips for starting an exercise routine. Though exercise may seem **irrelevant** to a psychological disorder, its impact can make all the difference.

irrelevant: Not related to something else.

After meeting with her doctor, Beth started a walking routine that turned into slow jogging. She eventually started running and found that her physical progress toward fitness not only helped her body but her depression as well.

Diet and Dietary Supplements

Years ago, a famous advertising campaign slogan announced, "You are what you eat!" While that's not entirely true, what we eat can affect both our physical and mental health status.

Dr. Edward Drummond, in his book *The Complete Guide to Psychiatric Drugs*, uses the illustration of British sailors who contracted scurvy during their long voyages at sea. Sailors with the disease ended up with spongy gums and loosened teeth, all for lack of ascorbic acid, what we know today as vitamin C. Adding limes, which are rich in vitamin C, to the sailors' diets prevented the disease.

Yes, there is a connection between what we eat and drink and how we feel. Researchers over the last several years have determined that the chief cause of fatigue in most Americans is chronic dehydration—not getting enough to drink. Are you tired all the time? You may want to ask yourself if you're drinking enough water during the course of the day.

But diet doesn't only affect physical symptoms. It can affect our mental conditions, too. Drummond later notes in his book that not eating enough, nor balancing the right types of food, can worsen psychiatric symptoms.

One caution: dietary supplements (vitamins) and food replacements like energy bars or meal-replacement shakes are not a healthy substitute for a balanced diet. The key when making choices about

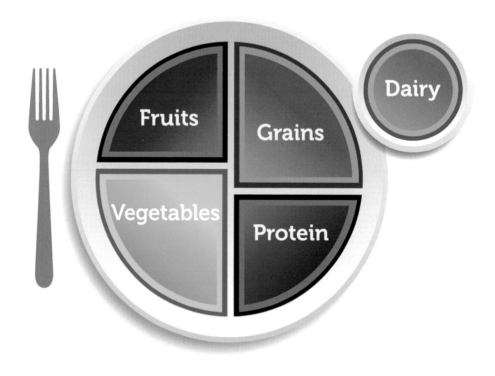

The U.S. government's MyPlate diagram provides a way to think visually about the foods we need to maintain healthy minds and bodies. According to MyPlate, half of the food on your plate should be fruits and vegetables. You should eat smaller amounts of whole grains and healthy proteins, along with dairy. Fats and sweets should not play a major role in a good diet. Unfortunately, many North Americans have more fatty and sugary foods in their diets than they do anything else. How does your diet compare to MyPlate?

what we eat is to get adequate, balanced nutrition. Make sure your body is getting the fuel it needs.

Psychotherapy

Diet and exercise can certainly affect our physical health and emotional outlooks, but they do little to change our ways of thinking or our behaving. Many alternate treatment strategies can help with our thought processes, attitudes, and actions. These can be summed up by the term psychotherapy.

Psychotherapy includes a number of common nondrug treatments for psychological disorders that work well when used in conjunction with psychiatric drug treatment. In fact, most psychiatrists would not recommend that psychiatric drugs be used alone; they would encourage patients on psychiatric drugs to pursue psychotherapy. Which kind? That depends on the patient and the psychological disorder.

Patients today have a wide variety of psychotherapy options from which to choose. Psychiatrist Edward Drummond lists several in his book:

- *Behavioral therapy* believes that a person's response to his surroundings can be changed by practice, planning, and performing certain assignments. Behavior therapy helped Katie, an eleven-year-old with OCD, overcome her fear of dirt. Her therapist told Katie to touch a small pile of dirt put on the kitchen table once a day for a week. Katie completed her assignment successfully, so the therapist then had Katie start pushing the dirt in circles around on the table once a day until she no longer felt anxious. This progressed to more and more assignments that increased Katie's ability to live normally and overcome her fear.
- *Cognitive therapy* involves thinking. It includes self-talk based on what you know to be true about your condition, your

surroundings, and your perceptions. When a depressed teenager says, "This problem is never going to go away," a cognitive therapist would say that the teen's perception, though it feels true and overwhelming, is not accurate. The reality is that the problem will eventually go away—someday. To help herself, this teen needs to do some self-talk to remind herself of what is true and not true in her situation.

- *Psychodynamic psychotherapy* assumes that many psychological disorders result from things that have happened in the patient's past. The patient may or may not be aware of these past events or conflicts and needs to meet weekly with a trained therapist to recall the events or to understand their impact. This kind of therapy can take years to produce change in the patient.

- *Interpersonal therapy* focuses on today, not the past. A psychiatrist or counselor works with the patient on problems the patient is currently experiencing with people in his life. They work together toward an understanding of how the patient's current relationships can help or hinder his psychological disorder. This treatment plan is usually shorter term (only a few months), and the patient and therapist meet weekly.

- *Group therapy* involves regular meetings (once a week or more) with other people who have a disorder in common. It can be very freeing to discover that you aren't "the only one" suffering from a mental illness. Anne, a sixteen-year-old high school junior, found great help from meeting with other teens who suffered with anxiety disorders. Her group therapy friends knew what it felt like to experience a panic attack so severe that you think you heart is literally going to jump out of your chest. She didn't have to explain her experience to them the way she did with her "normal" friends. These friends just "knew." What a relief it was to find someone who understood what she was going through. She wasn't alone!

Psychotherapy, especially when used while the patient is taking psychiatric medication, can help many people live happy, productive lives, even while battling psychological disorders. But psychotherapy can be very expensive since a psychiatrist, psychologist, or trained therapist is always involved. There is another avenue for alternate treatment that isn't quite so expensive: self-help groups.

Self-Help Groups

Self-help groups are exactly what they sound like they are: groups of people who are committed to helping themselves. The most common self-help groups today follow what are known as twelve-step recovery plans. The most famous and oldest of these groups is Alcoholics Anonymous (AA).

Group therapy allows people to share common fears and symptoms.

People with psychiatric disorders may feel as though their condition isolates them from everyone else. Therapy groups can relieve these feelings.

In 1935, a surgeon from Akron, Ohio, and stockbroker from New York City found themselves struggling to overcome addictions to alcohol. When they met, "Dr. Bob," the surgeon, had not completely stopped drinking; "Bill," the New Yorker, had been sober for some time. The positive, encouraging impact they had on each other was immediate. Together, they determined to help others who shared their disease. They started AA.

Viewing alcoholism as a problem of the mind, emotions, and body that someone could not face alone was unheard of in the 1930s. The two recovering alcoholics developed a new treatment plan that addressed all three areas. Over the next four years, one

When a person struggles with a psychiatric disorder, she may not be able to easily find a simple solution. Self-help groups can empower her to find the "key" to her own well-being.

hundred alcoholics stopped drinking as a result of their new treatment ideas. Today, nearly eighty years later, more than two million people worldwide call themselves members of AA.

The philosophy of many self-help groups is patterned after AA. They allow you to join using only your first name. They keep everything said in meetings confidential. Most groups believe that your disorder is something you cannot control or fix yourself, so they encourage spiritual beliefs that allow the patient to draw upon a "higher power." Regular meetings with others in the group provide support and encouragement, much like group therapy, except that self-help groups are free.

Alternative Medicines

"But what if I'm happy in therapy, don't need a self-help group, and am taking psychiatric drugs, but want to try herbs or vitamins instead? Are they safe?"

Many people who want to try alternatives to prescription drugs (including herbs, vitamins, and foreign concoctions not approved by the FDA) ask about alternative medicine safety. It's a good question.

Drummond lists seven issues to keep in mind when weighing the possibility of using alternative remedies. What follows is adapted from that list:

1. "Realize that a drug is a drug." Whether it comes from an FDA-approved capsule or your neighbor's herb garden, any chemical you take to influence your mind, thoughts, emotions, or body is considered a drug. The caffeine in Mountain Dew is every bit as much a drug as the prescription you pick up at the

Alcohol can be extremely destructive when it is abused. Self-help groups like Alcoholics Anonymous help individuals battle addiction and other psychological problems.

pharmacy. The vitamin E that athletes take to lessen muscle soreness is a drug, just as much as cold medicine is. Saint-John's-wort, the well-known herb people use for depression, works much the same way as Prozac, a prescription antidepressant. Just because it's not FDA approved or prescribed by your doctor doesn't mean that it's not a drug.

2. "Realize that 'natural' is neither good nor bad." Just because something is labeled natural doesn't make it any healthier for you. Certain kinds of mushrooms that grow in the wild are clearly natural by anyone's definition, but if eaten they can kill. Beware of false thinking that says, "Natural is better."

3. "Educate yourself about the evidence." When we looked at ways to lessen the risks of taking psychotropic drugs in chapter four, we said to "be informed." The same could be said of FDA-approved drugs or alternative remedies. Whatever you are considering taking for a psychiatric disorder, learn as much as you can about the drug's benefits and risks. FDA-approved psychiatric drugs *and* alternative medicines have benefits and risks. It's important to learn about them.

4. "Don't fall for 'It worked for him, it'll work for me.'" Everyone is different. Just because an alternative treatment, or an FDA-approved drug for that matter, works for someone else doesn't mean it will work for you. That would be like saying that since size twelve sneakers work for your friend, they will work for you, even though you only wear a size nine. The same treatment just won't fit everyone because our bodies aren't the same. Your diagnoses may be different. Your body chemistries may be different. Your genetic makeup is certainly different. Treatment plans don't come in "one size fits all" packages. That's why it's so important to consult with your doctor so she can prescribe the best treatment plan for you.

5. "Know that alternative remedies have side effects." Every drug, whether it's FDA approved or an alternative remedy,

Homeopathic Treatment for Psychiatric Disorders

Homeopathy is a form of alternative medicine that looks at disease and disorders from a very different perspective from conventional medicine. It treats a person's entire physical and mental being, rather than dividing a patient into various symptoms and disorders. Homeopathic medicine uses tiny doses to stimulate the body's ability to heal itself. In some cases, these doses may be administered only once every few months or years. Homeopathic practitioners believe their approach offers safe, natural alternatives that can supplement or replace conventional pharmaceutical treatment for psychiatric problems. Homeopathic medicines have few side effects, unlike the strong chemicals used for psychiatric drugs.

can cause adverse reactions. The advantage here falls to FDA-approved drugs. We've seen how the FDA requires drug sponsors to spend years testing for and reporting on various side effects. Because of the rigorous approval process most FDA-approved drugs go through to be approved, we know much more about their potential side effects. No such testing is done on alternative remedies (including herbs and vitamins). Side effects of these drugs just aren't known.

6. "Pick the right dosage." It's hard to figure out the right dosage to take for many alternative remedies. Why? Because most aren't regulated through their production process. The strength of one brand of herb could be much stronger or

much weaker than another brand. Since we are individuals with varying body chemistries, what works in one person may or may not work in another. Without clinical trials, it's impossible to adequately predict the correct dosages, so it's pretty much trial and error on the patient's part. This can be dangerous, since it is possible to overdose on natural remedies every bit as much as it is possible to overdose on prescription drugs.

7. "Inform your physician." Whatever you decide to do about drug treatment, it's essential that you discuss your treatment plans and decisions with your family doctor and your psychiatrist or psychologist. Drugs can interact with each other, no matter what kind they are or where they come from. While FDA-approved drug labeling (the package insert) describes these interactions, alternative remedies do not. Your doctor may be aware of dangerous interactions, even herb-to-herb, that will help you avoid running into trouble and may even save your life.

"If alternative medicines provide greater risks, in some cases, than FDA-approved drugs, why would someone want to take them?" That is another good question.

There are several reasons for trying alternate medicines. One of the most important is that not all FDA-approved drugs are approved for people of all ages. In other words, the FDA will sometimes approve a drug for use in adults, but not for use in children or teens. Because child, adolescent, and adult physiologies vary, drugs can impact their bodies differently. What is safe for an adult's body could be dangerous for a teen or a child. The FDA will approve a drug for use only in the patient group the drug safely treats. When a drug is approved for adults, but not children or teens, it means the drug is safe for adults, but it may pose dangers for non-adults. In some cases, the FDA cannot approve a drug's usage for teens or children simply because the drug was tested only on adults; the FDA cannot predict how adolescents and children might respond to the medication. Some doctors

Alternative remedies use natural substances—but these substances contain chemicals, just as conventional drugs do. Because these "natural" cures have not been approved by the FDA, they may provide greater risks to the consumer.

Kava may promote emotional well-being.

may feel the drug is safe for teens—but the FDA does not have the research to back its official approval.

Not having a drug approved for a certain age group isn't the only reason to try alternative treatments. Patients may have tried treatment with FDA-approved psychiatric drugs, but the drugs didn't work. Or a patient may have tried FDA-approved drugs that did work, but experienced adverse reactions severe enough to discontinue treatment. Some people try alternative medicines because they have no other choice.

If you are one of these people, remember: alternative medi-cines (herbs, vitamins, dietary supplements, natural remedies, medicinal teas, etc.) are still drugs. Most medical professionals would encourage you to use the same cautious approach to taking alternative medicines as you would to taking FDA-approved drugs. There are no magic pills.

Someone with schizophrenia may hear voices telling him destructive messages. Psychiatric medication may stop this disturbing phenomenon.

Chapter Six

A Case Study in Psychosis and Psychiatric Treatment

Nicholas started hearing voices when he was eighteen years old. At first he thought he heard laughing—like groups of kids sniggering at him. But the laughing turned to mocking.

"You're so stupid."

"You don't do anything right."

"You're nothing but a loser."

Nick would sometimes shake his head to try to make the voices stop, but they always seemed to echo in his mind. He tried talking back to the voices, but that didn't work either. He tried to ignore the voices, but they only grew louder. Then the voices started telling him to doing crazy things.

"Jump!" one voice insisted when Nicholas stood at the top of the stairs or near a window.

"Drive into that telephone pole!" another commanded when Nick drove to work one day.

"Stab your hand," a third voice urged when he sliced a bagel or did the dishes.

"Hit him!" said still another when Nick got angry with his dad.

The voices grew louder and stayed longer. They scared Nicholas, tormented him, and wouldn't leave him alone. What was Nick going to do?

To understand just how far treatment for psychological disorders has come through the centuries, and to summarize just how important the FDA approval process is for providing safe new psychiatric drugs, let's take a brief look at how Nicholas might have been treated over the years.

Nick's Treatment Through Time

Twelve thousand years ago, Nick would have had his head bored with a drill or stake to release the spirits that plagued his troubled soul.

Four thousand years ago, about the time of the ancient Egyptians, healers would have treated Nick's illness as a physical illness. They might have given him herbs or spices to ease his suffering. In later Egypt they may have attributed his mental breakdown to a loss of money, honor, or reputation. Healers would have encouraged Nick to make a sacrifice to the gods or commit suicide (an acceptable, even honorable way to die at the time).

In 400 BCE, the Greeks would have attributed Nicholas's malady to "black bile"—one of four substances thought to make up the body, which called for a physical treatment, not a spiritual cure.

In ages past, some people attributed psychological disturbances to evil spirits that came to a person during his sleep.

In early Rome, some two thousand years ago, philosophers and physicians would have quarantined Nicholas; they believed that mental illness spread by breathing bad air. They may have also called for a musician to soothe his inner turmoil. Music was considered a cure.

During the Middle Ages, most people believed that the mentally ill were possessed by the devil or his demons. Young Nicholas would have been chained in leg and wrist irons and beaten or tortured to drive the evil demons away. In later years, religious zealots would have burned the young man as a witch.

In the 1600s, London, England's notorious Bedlam Hospital may have provided a fate worse than death. Nick would have been shackled to a wall in a filthy dungeon and put on public display. For a fee, people could gawk at the unkempt soiled madman, throw things at him, or ridicule and taunt him. Mental illness was great entertainment for London's high society.

This painting by William Hogarth portrays the interior of Bedlam, a famous London hospital for the insane.

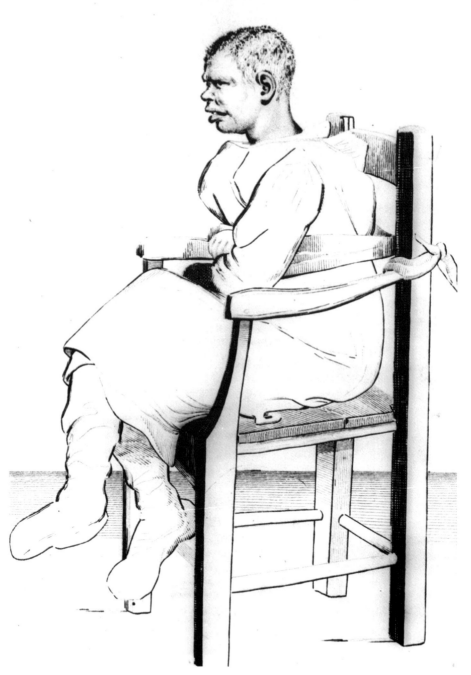

In the 1700s, many psychiatric patients were locked away for life.

A hundred years later, in the mid-1700s, our sad friend's family would have locked him away for life and forgotten him. Or they might have left him to starve on the streets. His family would have abandoned him because mental illness in the family was considered a deep, dark shame.

By the late 1700s and early 1800s, doctors and researchers began to realize that mental illness was a physical disease, so institutions were established to care for the mentally ill. Perhaps our Nicholas would have been taken to America's first psychiatric hospital. Opened by psychiatrist Benjamin Rush in 1769, the Virginia hospital made huge strides in the humane treatment of people like Nick. Patients with psychological disorders would no longer be whipped, chained, or put in straightjackets. They used other, more humane ways of confinement. But they would not have used drugs. Psychiatric drugs hadn't yet been discovered.

Fast-forward fifty years to the nineteenth century. Nick might have received the earliest psychiatric drug treatments in America.

By the 1900s, psychiatric patients were being treated in hospitals with more humane practices than in early centuries.

Key Protections Provided to Patients by the FDA

Because of the FDA, people living in the United States today can be confident that:

- Labeling on drugs (and food) is complete and accurate.
- FDA-approved medicines are safe.
- FDA-approved medicines are effective.
- Doctors aren't allowed to test drugs on patients without a patient's informed consent.

Doctors may have given him morphine, which most certainly would have sedated him (calmed him down or put him to sleep), but would not have eliminated the voices in his head. Maybe in desperation he would have tried a worthless patent medicine cure, which might have done nothing, made him worse, or poisoned him. The FDA hadn't yet established laws about drug labeling or safety.

It wouldn't be until the 1950s that Nick would have access to the first effective psychiatric medicines. By this time, FDA regulations required package labels to reveal what medicines contained, so Nick could be fairly sure that the drugs he took were safe. But would they work? There was only one way to find out. Doctors in the 1950s might have tested experimental drugs on Nick, with or without his knowledge (no laws forbade them from doing so). If medication didn't work, they might have performed an experimental frontal lobotomy. Poor Nick. Though he wasn't chained, he was still at the mercy of the doctors.

frontal lobotomy: Surgical removal of the front section of the brain as a treatment for mental illness.

Today medication plays a major role in the treatment of patients in psychiatric hospitals.

He didn't have the benefit of FDA consent protection laws passed in 1962.

In 1952, Thorazine, a drug used to treat voices like those Nick heard, was discovered. It would have helped Nick tremendously, but not without cost. Thorazine caused its patients to make awkward, embarrassing facial expressions and movements at unpredictable times. But this new drug helped tame hallucinations, which paved the way for future drugs to treat psychiatric disorders. The first antidepressants would be developed in the same decade, and over the next thirty years psychiatric patients would have dozens of brands and treatment protocols from which to choose. Nick might have tried one.

protocols: A detailed plan of treatment or experimentation.

The 1960s brought FDA regulations requiring patients to give informed consent before being used in human drug testing. Nick would no longer be a guinea pig without his knowledge and permission.

At the same time, the FDA required medicine manufacturers to prove that their drugs were not only safe and labeled accurately, but that they worked. Now the medications Nick tried had a better chance of working—they'd been tried and proven effective. Nick's position was improving by leaps and bounds.

How sad it must have been to be a person with a psychiatric disorder living during any of these eras. Can you imagine the fear, the horror, the confusion, or shame? Nicholas, however, wasn't born in any of those times. Luckily for Nick, he lives at the start of the twenty-first century—a time when we know and understand far more about the brain, how it functions, and how psychological disorders and their symptoms can best be treated.

So how did our current-day Nick fare? His symptoms became too much for him to handle on his own.

Though he hesitated to tell his parents about his voices (the voices told him not to tell), they were beginning to scare him. He was afraid he might harm himself or someone else. Nick told his mother and father. Right away, his parents called the doctor and set up an appointment with a psychiatrist. The diagnosis? Schizophrenia.

Once diagnosed, Nick could choose from several treatment options. If he really felt like he might hurt himself or others, he could voluntarily choose to stay in a psychiatric hospital for a short time until medications brought the voices under control. If he thought he could live safely at home with his parents, but needed intensive support, he could try a program where he slept at home but spent his days in a structured psychiatric program. Nick also had a variety of drug treatment options available to him.

Before Nicholas started on medication, he discussed different drug options with his doctor. He considered things like the drug's track record (how effective the drug had been in treating symptoms like his in the past) and the dosing schedule he would have to follow (how often would he have to take the drug and how disruptive the dosing regimen would be to his everyday life). He asked about the likelihood of side effects and how severe they might be. All of these

It is important to discuss various drug options with the prescribing practitioner.

The prescribing practitioner should closely monitor her patients' physical condition.

questions would have been unanswerable in the past, but because of FDA regulations, guidelines, and procedures, Nick could get the answers he needed. After a few more questions and much discussion with his doctor, they decided together on a treatment plan.

Unlike decades and centuries ago, Nick's psychiatrist was able to prescribe a safe, FDA-approved drug that could help him, one that had minimal side effects and controlled Nick's voices, though it was not a cure.

Nick is only one of millions of North Americans who suffer each year from a diagnosable psychological disorder. Treatment options for people with psychological disorders continue to improve as we learn more about the brain and discover new, safe, effective drugs. Now more than ever, a patient with mental illness can choose from a wide array of psychiatric drugs or alternative medicines. Though once doomed to a life of misery, despair, and isolation, people with psychiatric disorders have every reason to expect to live full, meaningful, well-adjusted lives. There is reason to hope and look forward to the future, largely because of the advances of science and the regulatory protection given patients by the FDA.

Further Reading

Diamond, Ronald J. *Instant Psychopharmacology: Up-to-Date Information about the Most Commonly Prescribed Drugs for Emotional Health* (2nd ed.). New York: W. W. Norton, 2009.

Drummond, Edward H. *The Complete Guide to Psychiatric Drugs: Straight Talk for Best Results*. New York: John Wiley and Sons, 2006.

Gitlin, M. J. *The Psychotherapist's Guide to Psychopharmacology* (2nd ed.). New York: Free Press, 2007.

Hicks, James Whitney. *50 Signs of Mental Illness*. New Haven, Conn.: Yale University Press, 2005.

Kaufman, Miriam. *Overcoming Teen Depression: A Guide for Parents*. Buffalo, N.Y.: Firefly, 2001.

Partner, Daniel. *Disorders First Diagnosed in Childhood*. Philadelphia: Chelsea House, 2001.

Wilens, Dr. Timothy E. *Straight Talk about Psychiatric Medications for Kids*. New York: The Guilford Press, 2008.

For More Information

American Academy of Child and Adolescent Psychiatry
www.aacap.org

Mental Health America
www.mentalhealthamerica.net

Substance Abuse and Mental Health Services Administration
www.samhsa.gov

National Mental Health Information Center
www.mentalhealth.org

United States Food and Drug Administration
www.fda.gov

The United States Surgeon General's Report on Mental Health
profiles.nlm.nih.gov/ps/retrieve/ResourceMetadata/NNBBHS

Publisher's Note:
The websites listed on this page were active at the time of publication. The publisher is not responsible for websites that have changed their address or discontinued operation since the date of publication. The publisher will review and update the websites upon each reprint.

Index

About the Author & Consultants

Joan Esherick is a full-time author, freelance writer, and professional speaker who lives outside of Philadelphia, Pennsylvania. Joan has contributed dozens of articles to national print periodicals, written spiritual and educational books, and speaks nationwide.

Mary Ann McDonnell, Ph.D., R.N., is the owner of South Shore Psychiatric Services, where she provides psychiatric services to children and adolescents. She has worked as a psychiatric nurse at Franciscan Hospital for Children and has been a clinical instructor for Northeastern University and Boston College advanced-practice nursing students. She was also the director of clinical trials in the pediatric psychopharmacology research unit at Massachusetts General Hospital. Her areas of expertise are bipolar disorder in children and adolescents, ADHD, and depression.

Donald Esherick has worked in regulatory affairs at Rhone-Poulenc Rorer, Wyeth Pharmaceuticals, Pfizer, and Pharmalink Consulting. He specializes in the chemistry section (manufacture and testing) of investigational and marketed drugs.